Elizabeth J. Cotton

Young folks' History of Greece and Rome

Elizabeth J. Cotton

Young folks' History of Greece and Rome

ISBN/EAN: 9783744782944

Printed in Europe, USA, Canada, Australia, Japan

Cover: Foto ©Paul-Georg Meister /pixelio.de

More available books at **www.hansebooks.com**

HISTORY OF GREECE AND ROME

USED IN 7B GRADE

INDIANAPOLIS PUBLIC SCHOOLS

COMPILED BY

ELIZABETH J. COTTON

INDIANAPOLIS
THE BOWEN-MERRILL CO.
1898

To Teachers

This work is intended to furnish materials for the foundation of the study of the history of Greece and Rome, and references for more extended reading.

HISTORY OF GREECE.

THE LAND AND THE PEOPLE.

Physical Greece.—Ancient Greece, or Hell′as, was the country of the Helle′nes. It was not restricted to the peninsula south of the Cambu′nian Mountains and the adjacent islands, but wherever the Hellenes settled, there was Hellas. Even the Hellenic colonies in Asia Minor, Italy, and the isles of the Æge′an and Mediterranean, were styled "patches of Hellas." Taken as a whole, Hellas was about the size of the state of Maine.

Greece, the peninsula, is separated by abrupt mountain walls into a number of isolated districts, each of which in ancient times became a state. Each valley developed its own peculiar life, hence the fragmentary character of its political history. The Hellenic states never coalesced to form a single nation.

"The peninsula is, by reason of deep arms and bays of the sea, converted into what is in effect an archipelago. No spot in Greece is forty miles from the sea. Hence its people were easily tempted to a sea-faring life. The islands, strewn with seeming carelessness through the Ægean Sea, were 'stepping-stones' which invited the earliest settlers of Greece to the delightful coast country of Asia Minor, and thus blended the life of the opposite shores. Intercourse with the old civilization of Egypt and Phœnicia stirred the naturally quick and versatile Greek intellect to early and vigorous thought."

Again, the beauty of Grecian scenery, of the blue skies, laughing rills, rugged mountains, and blue Mediterranean, inspired many of the most striking passages of her poets, making the Greeks a nation of artists. "The scenery of Greece was in direct contrast to the tame features of the Nile and Euphrates." The germs of culture transmitted to the West from the East would have lain dormant, or have developed into less perfect forms, without the quickening power of the Greek genius. "It was a case of good seed falling into good ground, and it brought forth a hundred fold."—*Compiled from Myers.*

The Hellenes.—There were four tribes—Ionian, Dorian, Achæan and Æolian—dwelling in these little states, and, though they often quarreled among themselves, yet they claimed to be members of a single family; all were descended, according to their fabled genealogy, from the common progenitor, Hellen, the son of Deucalion, the Grecian Noah. All those nations whose speech they did not understand they called "barbarians." Through the testimony of language, we do know that the Hellenes belonged to the great Aryan family; but their ancestors and those of the Romans, after they had separated from the other Aryan peoples, lived together a considerable time before they parted company. Some think the home where they lived as an undivided family was Phrygia in the northwest corner of Asia Minor, and that from that station successive bands of emigrants gradually spread themselves over Greece and the shores and islands of the Ægean.—*Compiled from Myers.*

Oriental Immigrants.—According to their own tradition they are indebted to Oriental immigrants for the introduction of the arts and culture of the East.

From Egypt, legend affirms, came an Egyptian colony, bringing with it the arts, learning, and priestly wisdom of the Nile valley. Ce'crops, the leader of the colony, is said to have founded Athens in 1556 B. C., and placed it under the protection of an Egyptian goddess, whose Greek name was Athena. "From the same land Dan'aus is also said to have come with his fifty daughters and to have built the city of Argos. (See *Miss Yonge's Young Folks' History of Greece.*) From Phœnicia, Cadmus brought the letters of the alphabet and founded the city of Thebes."—*Compiled from Myers.*

(Read stories of Euro'pa and Cadmus in "Little Arthur's History of Rome.")

About 1350 B. C., Pelops, the son of a king of Phrygia, a country in Asia Minor, settled in that part of Greece which was afterwards called, for him, Peloponnesus. There he married the daughter of one of the native princes, whom he succeeded to the throne. Agamemnon and Menelaus, heroes of the Trojan War, were descended from this Phrygian adventurer.—*Compiled from S. G. Goodrich.*

THE HEROIC AGE.

The Heroes.—"The Greeks believed that their ancestors were heroes of divine or semi-divine lineage. Every tribe, district, city, and village, even, preserved traditions of its heroes, whose wonderful exploits were commemorated in song and story. Among the most noted of the heroes are Hercules, Theseus, king of Athens, and Minos, king of Crete."—*Myers.*

(Read Francillon's "Gods and Heroes," Charlotte Yonge's "Young Folks' History of Greece," "Greek Stories," by Guerber, Church's "Stories of Homer," Kingsley's "Greek Heroes.")

"Hercules, a Theban prince, was another of the descendants of Pelops. The numerous and extraordinary feats of strength and valor of Hercules excited the admiration of his contemporaries, and, being afterwards exaggerated and embellished by the poets, caused him at length to be regarded as a person endowed with supernatural powers, and even to be worshiped as a god.

"According to the poets, Hercules was the son of the god Jupiter, and of Alcmena, daughter of the king of Mycenæ. His mother married Amphitryon, king of Thebes, by whom the infant Hercules was adopted as his son. While yet a child in the cradle, he is fabled to have crushed to death two snakes which the goddess Juno had sent to destroy him. After he grew up he performed many heroic and extraordinary actions, commonly called 'labors.' Among these was the destruction of a dreadful lion, by clasping his arms around its neck and thus choking it to death.

"Another of the fabled labors of Hercules was his destroying the hydra of Lerna. This was a monstrous seven-headed serpent, which haunted the small lake of Lerna in Argolis, and filled with terror the inhabitants of the whole of that part of the country. Hercules dauntlessly attacked it, and struck off several of its heads with his club. But these wonderful heads were no sooner beaten off than others grew out, so that it seemed an impossibility to kill a monster whose injuries were so quickly repaired. At last, one of the companions of Hercules having, at the hero's request, seared with a hot iron the necks of the hydra as fast as each decapitation was accomplished, it was found that the heads did not afterwards grow out again, and Hercules was thus enabled to complete the destruction of the reptile."—S. G. Goodrich.

(See Niebuhr and Miss Yonge.)

Argonautic Expedition.—"During the life-time of Hercules, 1263 B. C., Jason, a prince of Thessaly, made a voyage to Colchis, a country on the eastern side of the Euxine or Black Sea. His enterprise was afterwards greatly celebrated under the name of the Argonautic Expedition, from Argo, the vessel in which he sailed. This ship is generally referred to by the ancients as the first that ever ventured on a long voyage. It is uncertain what was the real object of the expedition, although it seems probable that, as Colchis was rich in mines of gold and silver, Jason and his companions, among whom were Hercules and several other persons of distinction, were actuated by a desire to rob the country of some of its valuable metals. The poets, however, tell us a different story. Phryxus and Helle, the son and daughter of Athamas, king of Thebes, being compelled, according to the poetic account, to quit their native country to avoid the cruelty of their step-mother, mounted on the back of a winged ram with a fleece of gold, and were carried by this wonderful animal through the air towards Colchis, where an uncle of theirs, named Æetes, was king. Unfortunately, as they were passing over the strait now called Dardanelles, which connected the Ægean Sea with the Propontis, or Sea of Marmora, Helle became giddy, and, falling into the water, was drowned. From her, says the fable, the strait was in future named the Hellespont, or Sea of Helle.

"When Phryxus arrived in Colchis, he sacrificed his winged ram to Jupiter, in acknowledgment of the divine protection, and deposited its golden fleece in the same deity's temple. He then married the daughter of Æetes, but was afterwards murdered by that king, who wished to obtain possession of the golden fleece. To avenge Phryxus's death, Jason, who was his relation, undertook the expedition to Colchis, where, after performing several marvelous exploits, he not only obtained the golden fleece, but persuaded Medea, another daughter of King Æetes, to become his wife, and to accompany him back to Greece."—*S. G. Goodrich.*

Theseus.—" In the year 1234 B. C., Theseus came to the throne of Athens. He was one of the most renowned characters in the heroic age of Greece, not only on account of his warlike achievements, but from his political wisdom."—*S. G. Goodrich.*

(See Bulfinch and Francillon.)

Homer.—The real history of Greece does not begin before the eighth century B. C. All that lies back of that belongs to the mythical or Heroic Age. Toward the close of the Heroic Age there were a great many songs and verses composed, telling of the gods and heroes. Singers and poets were entertained by the kings, and welcomed by all, as they chanted to the harp or the lyre the stories of the great forefathers of their hosts. Their favorite themes were the exploits of those heroes whose adventures have been familiar in each succeeding age to the youth of every civilized land, namely: "The Twelve Labors of Hercules," "The Argonautic Expedition in Search of the Golden Fleece," the "Hunt of the Calydonian Boar," and the "Siege of Troy."

The greatest of these singers was the blind poet Homer, whose songs of the wrath of Achilles and the wanderings of Ulysses were loved and learned by every one. "According to tradition, Homer was a schoolmaster of Asia Minor, living in the 9th or 10th century, B. C. Becoming weary of confinement he traveled widely, became blind, but still wandered, singing his verses which were to become immortal. Notwithstanding the verdict of late authorities who consider the "Iliad" and "Odyssey" to have been formed out of the fragmentary verses of many bards, it is probable that the poems will always be known as Homer's "Iliad" and "Odyssey." His fame among his countrymen is attested by the well-known Greek epigram which reads : —

" 'Several rival towns contend for Homer dead,
Through which the living Homer begged his bread.' "
—*Compiled from Miss Yonge.*

(Read Brook's Story of "Iliad" and "Odyssey," Lamb's "Adventures of Ulysses."

RELIGION OF THE GREEKS.

Gods and Goddesses.—The Greeks were not trained in the knowledge of God like the Israelites, but originated a religion for themselves. They made wonderful stories of the powers of nature, the sky, sun, moon, stars, and clouds, as if they were gods. They thought there were twelve greater gods and goddesses who lived on Mount Olympus and ruled the affairs of mortals.

Zeus, or Jupiter, the son of Saturn, was the chief of them all, and the ruler of earth and heaven.

Neptune, or Poseidon, was the Lord of the ocean (that is, the Mediterranean). *Pluto*, or Hades, was the lord of the world of the spirits of the dead. "Jupiter was always thought of by the Greeks as a majestic-looking man, with thick hair and beard, and with lightnings in his hand and an eagle by his side. The lightnings were forged by his crooked son *Vulcan*, the god of fire, whose smithies were in the volcanoes (so-called from his name), and whose workmen were the *Cyclops*, or Round Eyes— giants, each with one eye in the center of his forehead."
—*Charlotte Yonge.*

Athena.—"Once when Jupiter was hard-pressed by the Titans, a horrible race of giants, a dreadful pain in his head caused him to bid Vulcan strike it with his hammer. Then out darted Heavenly Wisdom, his beautiful daughter, Pallas Athena, or Minerva, fully armed. By her counsels he cast down the Titans and heaped their own mountains, Etna, Ossa, and Pelion, upon them. Whenever there was an earthquake, it was thought to be one of these giants struggling to be free. Pallas was also goddess of all woman's works, of spinning, weaving, and sewing."—*Charlotte Yonge.*

Juno was Jupiter's wife, the queen of the heavens.

(See stories of Gods and Goddesses. *Bulfinch, Francillon* and *Cox.*)

"*Mercury*, or Hermes, really meant the morning breeze. The story was told that he was born early in the morning in a cave, and, after he had slept a little while in his cradle, he came forth, and, finding the skull of a tortoise with the strings of the inwards stretched across it, he at once began to play, and formed the first lyre. He was so swift that he was the Messenger of Jupiter, and he is always represented with wings on his cap and sandals; but, as the wind not only makes music but blows things away unawares, so Mercury came to be viewed as the god of thieves."—*Charlotte Yonge.*

Iris.—Another messenger of the gods, belonging chiefly to Juno, was Iris, the rainbow, a recollection of the bow in the clouds.

Apollo and Diana.—The god and goddess of light were the glorious twin brother and sister Phœbus Apollo, the lord of the day, and Diana, queen of the night. The beams or rays of light were their arrows, and so Diana was a huntress, always in the woods with her nymphs. The moon belongs to Diana, and is her car, the sun in like manner to Apollo. "In the far East the lady Dawn, *Aurora* or Eos, opened the gates with her rosy fingers, and out came the golden car of the sun, with glorious white horses driven by Apollo, attended by the Hours strewing dew and flowers. It passed over the arch of the heavens to the ocean again on the west, and there

Aurora met it again in fair colors, took out the horses and let them feed."

Phaeton.—Apollo had a son, named Phaeton, who once begged to be allowed to drive the chariot of the sun for just one day: "Apollo yielded, but poor Phaeton had no strength or skill to guide the horses in the right curve. At one moment they rushed to the earth and scorched the trees; at another they flew up to heaven, and would have burned Olympus had not Jupiter cast his thunderbolt at the rash driver and hurled him down into a river, where he was drowned. His sisters wept till they were changed into poplar trees, and their tears hardened into amber drops."—*Compiled from Miss Yonge.*

Muses.—"Mercury gave his lyre to Apollo, who was the true god of music and poetry, and under him were nine nymphs—the Muses, daughters of memory—who dwelt on Mt. Parnassus, and were thought to inspire all noble and heroic song, all poems in praise of the gods and brave men."—*Compiled from Miss Yonge.*

Venus was the goddess of beauty. "She was said to have risen out of the sea, as the sunshine touched the waves, with her golden hair dripping with spray. Her favorite home was in myrtle groves, where she drove her car, drawn by doves, attended by the Graces, and by multitudes of little winged children called Loves; but there was generally said to be one special son of hers, called Love—Cupid in Latin, Eros in Greek,—whose arrows when tipped with gold made people fall in love, and when tipped with lead made them hate one another. Her husband was the ugly, crooked smith, Vulcan,—

perhaps because pretty ornaments came of the hard work of the smith; but she never behaved well to him, only coaxed him when she wanted something his clever hands could make. She was very fond of amusing herself with *Mars* (Ares), the god of war; another of the evil gods, for he was fierce, cruel, and violent. Where he went slaughter and blood were sure to follow him and his horrid daughter Bellona. His star was 'the red planet Mars,' but Venus had the beautiful clear one, which is the morning or evening star."—*Miss Yonge.*

"*Ceres* was the grave, motherly goddess of corn and all the fruits of the earth. *Persephone*, her daughter, was the flowers and fruit."—*Miss Yonge.*

(See Cox's story of Demeter.)

Vulcan, Hebe, and Ganymede.—" The twelve greater gods and goddesses had palaces on Olympus, and met every day in Jupiter's court to feast on ambrosia, a food of life which made them immortal. Their drink was nectar, which was poured into their golden cups at first by Vulcan, but he stumbled and hobbled so with his lame leg that they chose, instead, the fresh and graceful Hebe, the goddess of youth, till she was careless, and one day fell down, cup, nectar, and all. The gods thought they must find another cup-bearer, and, looking down, they saw a beautiful youth, Ganymede, watching his flocks upon Mt. Ida, so they sent Jupiter's eagle down to fly away with him and bring him to Mt. Olympus. They gave him some ambrosia to make him immortal and establish him as their cup-bearer. The gods were also thought to feed on the smoke and smell of sacrifices people offered up to them on earth, and to favor those mortals who offered them most sacrifices of animals and incense."—*Miss Yonge.*

Early Civilization.—"The poems of Homer furnish us with a pretty accurate picture of the political state of Greece at the time of the Trojan War. Sparta and Mycenæ appear to have been the most powerful states; they were both governed by princes of the Pelopid race, which had just arrived at the height of its power. The different tribes were ruled by hereditary chieftains, who combined the offices of leader in war and judge in peace; but the authority possessed by the rulers does not appear to have been despotic.

"The people dwelt in cities, but still were chiefly engaged in cultivating the land and tending cattle; commerce, however, had not been neglected, and the art of navigation was rapidly advancing, especially among the Greeks on the eastern coast.

"After a protracted siege of ten years, Troy fell; but the captors had no great reason to rejoice in their success; some of their bravest warriors had fallen in the contest, others perished in the voyage home; the greater part of the remainder found, at their return, strangers in possession of their throne, and either fell beneath the daggers of the usurpers or were compelled to seek new homes in a foreign land. But to Greece in general this war produced at least one beneficial result: it kindled one common national spirit, a spirit which, in spite of feuds and dissensions, was never wholly extinguished. From the time of the Trojan war downwards, the Hellenes looked upon themselves as constituting one people."—*Dr. Goldsmith.*

Dorian Migration.—About 1104 B. C., the Dorians, who had been dwelling in the barren mountain region of the north of Greece, sought new homes in the fertile valleys of the Peloponnesus. They are said to have been led by the Heracleidæ, the descendants of Hercules, who had been driven out of the Peloponnesus by the family of Pelops. The invaders were everywhere successful, conquering the Achæans and occupying the cities of Argos, Corinth and Sparta.

Colonization.—"A part of the Achæans fled northward, dispossessing the Ionians, who crossed the Ægean to Asia Minor." "Here and on the adjacent islands they founded settlements, which grew into cities. Among these cities was Ephesus, renowned for its temple of Diana, one of the Seven Wonders of the ancient world."

"North of the Ionians, Æolian emigrants established twelve towns, while the Dorians themselves settled the southern coast and the adjacent island of Rhodes. Rhodes was celebrated for its Colossus, an immense image of Apollo, so placed as to bestride the entrance to the harbor. The Colossus was over one hundred feet high, and its thumb was so large that a man could not clasp it with his arms. When, after lying on the ground for centuries, it was removed, the metal that composed it loaded nine hundred camels.

"The Greeks also peopled the shores of the Euxine (Black Sea). They founded Byzantium (the modern Constantinople) in the east, Massilia (Marseilles) in the far west, and the rich Cyrene on the coast of Africa. Many Greek colonies were planted in lower Italy and Sicily, which received the name of Magna Græcia

(Mag'na Gre'-shea, Great Greece). The most important of these were the luxurious Tarentum in south Italy, and Syracuse on the island of Sicily."—*Quackenbos.*

Had it not been for the power of Carthage, a Phœnician city, the Greeks would have secured nearly the entire shore and transformed the Mediterranean into a "Grecian lake."

Wherever the Greek went he retained his individuality. The Hellenic language, manners and civilization were introduced by him into barbarian lands. The colonies seemed to gain a new impulse of life and progressed more rapidly than the mother country.

The Asiatic Greeks rapidly increased both in wealth and intelligence, while the history of the parent states in this early age exhibited nothing but a succession of petty wars. "In all the states except Epirus, hereditary royalty was abolished and a republican form of government adopted, which impressed upon the people a love of political freedom.

"Even at this early age, we find that Sparta was considered the chief of the Dorian, and Athens of the Ionian states."—*Dr. Goldsmith.*

Sparta.—"After the subjugation of Laconia, the people were divided into three classes: The Dorian conquerors, who became known as Spartans, and alone enjoyed political privileges; the Achæans or free inhabitants of the rural districts, who were allowed by the Spartans to occupy the worst of the lands, and to engage in commerce or the trades; and the Helots, consisting of captives and rebels reduced to slavery. The Helots were employed in agricultural pursuits, and treated with great brutality. They could even be put to death when they

became so numerous as to appear dangerous to the state."
—*Quackenbos.*

Lacedæmon, called also Sparta from its grain fields (sown land), was the Spartan camp. "The name Sparta was strictly applicable only to the citadel erected on a hill in the center of the city. Lacedæmon was a common name for the residences of the five Laconian tribes which were erected round the citadel. It was one of the largest cities in Greece, but being built in a straggling manner, was not so populous as several others. As the Spartans professed to despise the fine arts, their city did not contain any edifice of importance. There is nothing in the situation of Lacedæmon which would lead us to anticipate the eminence at which it arrived. The river Eurotas, on whose banks it stood, was celebrated for the clearness and salubrity of its waters, but it was not a navigable stream, and afforded no facilities for commerce. The fame of Sparta was owing to its political institutions, and not to its geographical position."
—*Dr. Goldsmith.*

In this city the Spartans (only nine thousand strong in the time of Lycurgus) lived in the midst of a hostile population, "like soldiers on guard."

Government.—"Sparta was in the beginning ruled by kings, but under the Heraclei'dæ two kings governed with equal authority. This change is said to have been owing to the following circumstance.: One of the kings had twin sons so very much alike that it was hardly possible to distinguish one from the other. The mother, equally attached to both, was desirous of advancing both to the throne. The people therefore invested both with sovereign power, and this form of government continued to exist for centuries.

"It was during this latter period that the Helots, or peasants of Sparta, were enslaved; for these people, having taken up arms in order to vindicate their right to the same privileges as the citizens enjoyed, were, after a violent struggle, subdued. To prevent the repetition of these and like disorders, to which this little state was subject, Lycurgus instituted his celebrated body of laws, which continued for a long time to render Lacedæmon at once the terror and the umpire of the neighboring kingdoms."—*Dr. Goldsmith.*

Lycurgus.—In the ninth century B. C., Lycurgus, a member of the royal family, after carefully studying the laws of foreign countries, framed for his own the constitution which now bears his name. "He traveled into Crete and afterwards into Asia, where he is said to have discovered the works of Homer. Thence he went into Egypt, and having made himself acquainted with the customs and institutions of the various countries through which he passed, he at length returned home."

Lycurgus retained the double monarchy but limited its power. Their authority was considerably diminished by a Senate and the Court of the Eph'ori, consisting of five members only, chosen annually from among the people. These had the power to arrest and imprison even the persons of their kings, if they acted in a manner unbecoming their station.

"In order to reconcile the people to a government in which they had no real share, Lycurgus adopted two expedients. These were, to divide all the lands of the state equally among the citizens and to abolish the use of money. The latter he accomplished by ordering that nothing but iron money should pass in exchange for any commodity. This coin, also, he made so heavy, and fixed at so low a rate, that a cart and two oxen were required to carry home a sum of twenty pounds sterling."

"To enforce the practice of temperance and sobriety, Lycurgus ordained that all the men should eat together in one common hall. Every one was obliged to send thither his provisions monthly, consisting of one bushel of flour, eight measures of wine, five pounds of cheese and two pounds and one-half of figs. Black broth was their favorite dish." Agis, a man of high rank, having returned from a successful expedition, ventured to send for his broth that he might partake of his meal at home with his wife. For this foolish show of sentiment he was punished by a heavy fine.—*Dr. Goldsmith.*

The Spartan Boy.—"To accustom the youth to early habits of discipline and obedience, Lycurgus took their education out of the hands of the parents and committed it to masters appointed by the state.

"So desirous was he of having a hardy and robust race of citizens, that such children as were born with any capital defect were not suffered to be brought up, but were exposed to perish in a cavern near Mt. Taygetus, and such as, upon a public view, were deemed sound and healthy, were adopted as children of the state, and delivered to their parents to be nursed with rigor and severity.

"From their tenderest years they were accustomed to make no choice in their eating ; not to be afraid in the dark, or when left alone ; not to be peevish or fretful ; to walk barefoot ; to lie on beds of rushes ; to wear the same clothes summer and winter ; and to fear nothing from their equals.

"At the age of seven they were taken from their parents and delivered over to the classes for a public education, where their discipline was yet more rigid and severe. They were still obliged to go barefoot, their heads were shaved, and they fought with one another naked.

"To enable them the better to endure bodily pain without complaining, they were annually whipped at the altar of Diana, and the boy that bore this punishment with the greatest fortitude was highly honored.

"In order to prepare them for the stratagems of war, they were permitted to steal from one another, but if they were caught in the act they were punished for their lack of dexterity. Plutarch tells us of one, who, having stolen a fox, and hid it under his coat, chose rather to let the animal tear out his vitals than to discover the theft.

"At twelve years of age they were removed into a higher class, where their labor and discipline was still more severe. They had now their skirmishes between small parties, and their mock fights between larger bodies.

"Such was the constant discipline of the minority, which lasted till the age of thirty, before which time they were not permitted to marry, to enter the army or to bear any office of state."—*Dr. Goldsmith.*

Spartan Girl.—"The discipline of the virgins was as severe as that of the young men. They were inured to a life of labor and industry till they were twenty years old, before which time they were not considered as marriageable. They had also their peculiar exercises. They ran, wrestled and pitched the bar, and performed all these feats before the whole body of the citizens.

"So masculine an education did not fail to bestow upon the Spartan women equal vigor of body and mind. They were bold, hardy, and patriotic, filled with a sense of honor, and a love of military glory.

"Some foreign women, in conversation with the wife of Leonidas, saying that the Spartan women alone knew how to govern the men, she boldly replied: 'The Spartan women alone are the mothers of men.' A mother was known to give her son a shield when going to battle with this gallant advice: 'Return with it, or return upon it.'"—*Dr. Goldsmith.*

Disappearance of Lycurgus.—"In order to render his law more lasting Lycurgus pretended that something was still wanting to the completion of his plan, and that it was necessary for him to go and consult the oracle at Delphi. In the meantime he persuaded his countrymen to take an oath for the strict observance of all his laws till his return, and then left Sparta with a firm resolution of never seeing it more.

"When he arrived at Delphi, he inquired of the oracle whether the laws he had made were sufficient to render the Lacedæmonians happy, and being told that they were, he sent his answer to Sparta, and then voluntarily starved himself to death. Others say that he died in Crete, ordered his body to be burned and his ashes to be thrown into the sea.

"Whichever of these was the case, he equally obliged his countrymen, by the oath they had taken, to observe his laws forever, which, indeed, they were sufficiently inclined to do from a conviction of their real and intrinsic merit."—*Dr. Goldsmith.*

THE SPARTAN'S MARCH.

FELICIA HEMANS.

[The Spartan considered himself too brave to need the inspiration of martial music to impel him to the conflict. Thucydides says: "The Spartans used not the trumpet in their march into battle, because they wished not to excite the rage of their warriors. Their charging step was made to the 'Dorian mood of flutes and soft recorders.'"]

'Twas morn upon the Grecian hills,
 Where peasants dressed the vines;
Sunlight was on Cithæron's rills,
 Arcadia's rocks and pines.

And brightly through his reeds and flowers
 Eurotas wandered by,
When a sound arose from Sparta's towers,
 Of solemn harmony.

Was it the hunter's choral strain
 To the woodland goddess poured?
Did virgin hands in Pallas' fane
 Strike the full-sounding chord?

But helms were glancing on the stream,
 Spears ranged in close array,
And shields flung back a glorious beam
 To the morn of a fearful day.

And the mountain echoes of the land
   Swelled through the deep blue sky;
While to soft strains moved forth a band
   Of men that moved to die.

They marched, not with the trumpet blast,
   Nor bade the horn peal out,
And the laurel groves, as on they passed,
   Rung with no battle shout.

They asked no clarion's voice to fire
   Their souls with an impulse high;
But the Dorian reed and the Spartan lyre
   For the sons of liberty!

And still sweet flutes their path around
   Sent forth Æolian breath;
They needed not a sterner sound
   To marshal them to death.

So moved they calmly to the field,
   Thence never to return,
Save bearing back the Spartan shield
   Or on it proudly borne.

Athens.—"North of the Peloponnesus, jutting out into the Ægean Sea, lay the rocky little Ionian State of Attica, with its lovely city Athens." There was a story that Neptune and Pallas Athene had striven for the guardianship of the city, and it was decided that the one who should produce the most precious gift for it should be its patron. "Neptune struck the earth with his trident, and there appeared a war-horse; but Pallas's touch brought forth an olive tree, and this was judged the most useful gift. The city bore her name; the tiny Athenian owl was her badge; the very olive tree she had bestowed was said to be the one which grew in the court of the Acropolis, a sacred citadel on a rock above the city, and near at hand was the temple called the Parthenon, or Virgin's shrine. Not far off was the Areop'agus, a hill of Ar'es or Mars, the great place for hearing causes, and doing justice; and below these there grew up a city filled with men brave as the Spartans, and far more thoughtful and wise, besides having a most perfect taste and sense of beauty."—*Miss Yonge.*

Kings.—During the Heroic Age, Athens was ruled by kings, like all the other Grecian cities. The most noted were Theseus and Codrus. The following legend is told of Codrus: At one time the Dorians invaded Attica, but were told by an oracle that they would never succeed if they slew the king of Athens. "Codrus heard of this oracle and devoted himself for his country. He found that in battle the Dorians always forebore to strike him, and he, disguising himself, went into the enemy's camp, quarreled with a soldier there, and thus caused himself to be killed so as to save his country. He was the last king. The Athenians would not have any one less noble sit in his seat, and appointed magistrates called Archons instead of kings."—*Miss Yonge.*

Lawgivers.—"Soon the Athenians fell into a state of misrule and disorder, and they called on a philosopher named Draco to draw up laws for them. Draco's laws were very strict, and for the least crime the punishment was death. Nobody could keep them, so they were set aside and forgotten, till a wise lawgiver, named Solon, undertook to draw up a fresh code of laws for them."—*Miss Yonge.*

"His first step was in favor of the poor, who had been grievously oppressed by the rich. It was difficult for a poor freeman to earn his subsistence, where the labor was principally performed by slaves; hence the poor were deeply in debt, and, at Athens, insolvent debtors, together with their wives and children, might be reduced into slavery, unless they could find other means of satisfying their creditors. He lowered the rate of interest, and took away the power over the person of the debtor.

"He divided the rich citizens into three classes and gave to them the privilege of holding office under the government. The poor were considered incapable of holding any employment in the state, but were given a right to vote in the assembly of the people.

"To counteract the influence of the popular assembly, Solon gave greater weight to the court of Areopagus and also instituted another council called the Senate, which consisted of one hundred from each tribe. It was increased to five hundred when the tribes were augmented to ten, afterward to six hundred.

"The court of the Areopagus had supreme control over the religion and morals of the state. The introduction of new deities, the regulation of public worship, and the education of youth, were objects of their peculiar care.

"To encourage industry he empowered the Areopagus to inquire into every man's method of procuring a livelihood, and to punish such as had no visible way of doing so. He ordained that a son should not be obliged to support his father in old age or necessity, if the latter had neglected to give him some trade or calling."—*Goldsmith.*

"At the head of the government were nine chief magistrates, who were called archons, and who were changed every three years. To work with these there was the Senate of four hundred aris'toi or nobles; but when war or peace was decided, the whole de'mos, or people, voted according to their tribes. After having set things in order, Solon is said to have been so annoyed by foolish questions on his schemes, that he went again on his travels. First he visited Mile'tus, in Asia Minor, then he went on to Lydia. This was a kingdom of Greek settlers in Asia Minor, where flowed that river Pactolus whose sands contained gold-dust from King Midas's washing, as the story went. The king was Crœsus, and his capital was Sardis."—*Miss Yonge.*

Tyrants.—After Solon's departure *Pisistratus*, a nephew of Solon, became absolute master of Athens. He headed the democratic party, was a good general, a persuasive orator and an able statesman. "Having presented himself in the market-place covered with blood, he assured the people that his life had been attempted by the nobility on account of his affection for the multitude; he therefore entreated that he should be permitted to arm a body-guard for his protection. This request being granted, ere long he seized the Acropolis and became the first tyrant of Athens." "The character of Pisistratus, as a ruler, merits every praise, he was a great encourager of learning, and during his administration Athens first became a literary city. He arranged the poems of Homer in their present order, from the detached portions sung by the wandering minstrels, and ordered that these sublime compositions should be publicly read at the solemn festivals.

"The sons of Pisistratus, *Hippias* and *Hipparchus* succeeded to the authority of their father, and for some time imitated his bright example. During their administration Athens first became remarkable for the splendor of its public buildings, and for the diligent cultivation of the fine arts. They erected Hermæ, columns surmounted with the head of Mercury, in the streets and squares, and inscribed on them moral sentences for the instruction of the people.

"The poets Anac'reon and Simon'ides were invited to their court, which was, indeed, the resort of all whom learning and genius made illustrious in Greece. Their reign, which lasted eighteen years, was justly termed 'the golden age of literature.'

"But the possession of such unlimited power by one family led to its abuse." Hipparchus, having offended a noble family, was assassinated. "The murder of his brother produced a great change in the character of Hippias; he became jealous, revengeful and cruel; in short, a tyrant in the worst sense of the word. His person and his government became alike odious. His enemies succeeded in having him denounced by the oracle at Delphi, and at length he was expelled by the assistance of the Spartans after his family had governed Athens for sixty-eight years." Hippias went over to the Persian court, and was henceforth the declared enemy of his native city, seeking aid in different quarters to re-establish his tyranny in Athens.—*Dr. Goldsmith.*

Democracy Established.—Shortly after Hippias was driven into exile the constitution was changed so as to give the people additional privileges. Ostracism was introduced, by which they banished obnoxious persons without trial. "If a man was thought to be dangerous to the state, the de'mos or people might sentence him to be banished. His name was written on an oyster shell, or on a tile, by those who wished him to be driven away, and these thrown into a great vessel. If they amounted to a certain number, the man was said to be ostracized, and forced to leave the city. This was sometimes done unjustly, but it answered the purpose of sending away rich men who became overbearing, and kept tyrants from rising up."—*Miss Yonge.*

At this time ten new tribes were organized in order to break up the four old ones. Fifty representatives were sent from each tribe to the senate. Ten generals, one from each tribe, commanded the army in daily turn. All free inhabitants of Attica obtained citizenship and met four times a month to deliberate and decide upon public questions. The democracy of Athens was thus established and in the words of Herodotus "the Athenian then grew mighty, and it became plain that liberty is a brave thing."

THE GRÆCO-PERSIAN WARS.

Cause.—"About the beginning of the fifth century B. C., the Ionian cities of Asia Minor rebelled against Darius, the Persian king, who had made them a part of his empire. Athens, the mother city, sent a fleet to aid them. This interference aroused the resentment of the Persian monarch, who, that he might be continually reminded of the insult, required a servant each day at dinner to exclaim three times, 'Master, remember the Athenians!'

"In 492 B. C., Darius dispatched an expedition to Greece, but it ingloriously failed. Before making a second attempt he sent envoys to demand from the several states earth and water, the usual tokens of submission. Many of the cities yielded; but Athens and Sparta answered by throwing the Persian heralds into pits and wells, and bidding them there find earth and water. These rival states now laid aside their jealousies, and prepared to meet the common foe."—*Quackenbos.*

Battle of Marathon.—"On came the army of Darius, commanded by his ablest generals, with directions to conquer Greece and bring back the Athenians in chains. Not dreaming of defeat, they took with them great blocks of marble to raise a monument in commemoration of their victory. After some successes in the Ægean sea, the Persians disembarked on the coast of Attica. Advancing to the plain of Marathon, 120,000 strong, they found an army of 10,000 Athenians drawn up to meet them. (490 B. C.)

"An urgent message had been sent to the Spartans for assistance. They at once prepared to aid their allies, but as their religious scruples prevented them from starting till the moon was full, they arrived too late to take part in the engagement. The honor of the day, however, was shared by the city of Platæa, which promptly sent all its fighting men to the support of the Athenians. The Greeks, under Miltiades, advanced to the charge at a quick pace; the Persians, withstanding their attack for a short time only, were soon in headlong flight. Six thousand of their number were left dead on the field, and the survivors returned to Asia in such of their galleys as escaped destruction.

"Miltiades became for a time the idol of the Athenians. But because of his failure in a subsequent expedition the ungrateful people cast him into prison, where he died of a wound."—*Quackenbos.*

(See Guerber's Greek Stories.)

EUCLES ANNOUNCING THE VICTORY OF MARATHON.
LETITIA LANDON.

[Eucles, the swiftest runner in Greece, ran with the tidings, and, reaching Athens, had breath only to tell the news when he fell dead in the street.]

He cometh from the purple hills,
 Where fight has been to-day;
He bears the standard on his hand,—
 Shout round the victor's way!
The sunset of a battle won
Is round his steps from Marathon.

Gather the myrtles near,
 And fling them on his path;
Take from her braided hair
 The flowers the maiden hath,
A welcome to the welcome one
Who hastens now from Marathon.

They crowd around his steps,
 Rejoicing, young and old;
The laurel branch he bears,
 His glorious tale hath told,
The Persian's hour of pride is done;
Victory is on Marathon.

She cometh with brightened cheek,
 She who all day hath wept
The wife and mother's tears
 Where her youngest infant slept;
The heart is in her eyes alone,—
What careth she for Marathon?

> But down on his threshold, down
>   Sinks the warrior's failing breath;
> The tale of that mighty field
>   Is left to be told by Death.
> 'Tis a common tale,—the victor's sun
> Sets in tears and blood o'er Marathon.

Ostracism of Aristides.—"Aristides the Just, and Themistocles, an aspiring statesman, now became prominent in Athens. But political differences sprang up between them, and through the intrigues of his rival Aristides was ostracised. While the people were voting, a stranger to Aristides, unable to write, handed him an oyster shell and asked him to place on it the name of Aristides. 'What harm has he done you?' said the honest patriot, complying with the request. 'None,' the man replied; 'but I am tired of hearing him called Aristides the Just.'

"Aristides left his country praying that nothing might happen which would make the Athenians regret his absence. His hopes, however, were not realized, for he was soon recalled to aid Themistocles in repelling a formidable Persian invasion. 'Themistocles,' he said, when they first met, 'let us be rivals, but let our strife be which best may serve our country.'"—*Quackenbos*.

Expedition of Xerxes.—"Xerxes, son of Darius, had long been raising a great army from all parts of the Persian Empire. It is stated that his forces numbered over two million of soldiers, besides slaves and attendants, and they drank rivers dry on their march.

"To reach Greece, the Persians had to cross the Hellespont. The first bridge constructed for their passage was broken up by a violent storm, which so enraged

Xerxes that he beheaded the workmen who had engaged in its erection, ordered the sea to be scourged with a monstrous whip, and had heavy chains thrown into it as symbols of its subjection to his control. Another bridge was soon built, and over it, for seven days and nights without cessation, poured the living throng, glittering with the wealth of the East—the largest army ever raised by man."—*Quackenbos*.

Battle of Thermopylæ (480 B. C.).—"Athens, meanwhile, under the direction of Themistocles, had prepared for the approaching struggle by equipping a powerful fleet. Sparta and many of the other states, forgetting their internal differences, united with her for the common defense.

"At the Pass of Thermopylæ, a narrow defile leading from Thessaly into Lower Greece, the Persian myriads were confronted by a handful of three hundred Spartans, under their king Leonidas, supported by about six thousand allies from the other states. Xerxes scornfully bade them give up their arms. 'Come and take them,' was the undaunted reply."—*Quackenbos*.

"And when it was observed that the Persian forces were so numerous that their very arrows would darken the sun, 'Then,' replied a Spartan, 'we shall fight in the shade.'

"Xerxes, provoked at these sarcasms, resolved to begin the attack immediately. The first assault was instantly repulsed with great slaughter. A body of ten thousand Persians, commonly known as the immortals, made another attempt to dislodge the Grecians, but with no better success." In a word, the Greeks maintained their ground against the whole power of the Persian army for two days, and the terrified Persians had to be driven to the assault with whips. On the third day a traitor conducted a body of twenty thousand Persians through a by-path across a mountain that overhung the straits.

"Leonidas, seeing the enemy in this situation, advised his allies to retire. 'As for myself and my fellow-Spartans,' said he, 'we are obliged by our laws not to fly: I owe a life to my country, and it is now my duty to fall in her defense.' Seven hundred Thespians gallantly resolved to share the fate of the Spartans. When the rest had retired, Leonidas exhorted his followers, in the most cheerful manner, to prepare for death. 'Come, my fellow-soldiers,' said he, 'let us dine cheerfully here, for to-night we shall sup with Pluto.' His men, upon hearing his determined purpose, set up a loud shout, as if they had been invited to a banquet, and resolved every man to sell his life as dearly as he could.

"The night began now to advance, and this was thought the most glorious opportunity of meeting death in the enemy's camp, as the darkness, by concealing the smallness of their numbers, would fill the Persians with greater consternation. Thus resolved, they made directly to the Persian tents, and in the silence of night had almost penetrated to the royal pavilion, with hopes of surprising the king. The Persians, incapable of distinguishing friend from foe, fell furiously upon each other, and rather assisted than opposed the Greeks. Thus success seemed likely to crown their bold but rash enterprise, had not morning dawn discovered the smallness of their numbers. They retreated back to the straits, and four times repulsed their Persian pursuers, but, while the victory was yet doubtful, the Persian detachment in their rear was seen descending from the hills. Nothing now remained but to sell their lives as dearly as possible ; abandoning, therefore, outer lines of defense, they formed themselves into a square and awaited the approach of their enemies. The Greeks were assailed on every side, yet not a man swerved from his post. The spears of the Greeks were blunted and shivered in the protracted contest. Leonidas, their leader, had fallen in the attack on the Persian camp, but his body, placed in the center of the diminished band was the rallying point of his exhausted soldiers. They sank at last beneath a mountain of darts, which formed the proudest testimony of their valor, and their most suitable monument. Of all the band, two only escaped whose names were Aristodemus and Panites. They were treated, in consequence, with such contempt on their return to Sparta, that Panites killed himself in despair, but Aristodemus bore it with fortitude, and recovered his honor by his gallant behavior on the battle of Platæa. The loss of the Persians at Thermopylæ is supposed to have amounted to twenty thousand men, among whom were two of the king's brothers.

"To perpetuate the memory of this wonderful exertion of valor two monuments were erected. The inscription on one commemorated the brave resistance made by a handful of Greeks against millions of Persians. The other was peculiar to the Spartans, and bore these words written by Simonides:"—*Dr. Goldsmith.*

"Go, stranger, and to Lacedæmon tell
That here, obeying her behests, we fell."—*Barnes.*

THE DEATH OF LEONIDAS.

GEORGE CROLY.

It was the wild midnight, a storm was on the sky;
The lightning gave its light, and the thunder echoed by.
The torrent swept the glen, the ocean lashed the shore;
Then rose the Spartan men, to make their bed in gore.

Swift from the deluged ground three hundred took the shield;
Then, in silence, gathered round the leader of the field!
All up the mountain's side, all down the woody vale,
All by the rolling tide waved the Persian banners pale.

And foremost from the pass, among the slumbering band,
Sprang King Leonidas, like the lightning's living brand.
Then double darkness fell, and the forest ceased its moan;
But there came a clash of steel, and a distant dying groan.

Anon, a trumpet blew, and a fiery sheet burst high,
That o'er the midnight threw a blood-red canopy,
A host glared on the hill, a host glared by the bay;
But the Greeks rushed onward still, like leopards in their play.

The air was all a yell, and the earth was all a flame,
Where the Spartan's bloody steel on the silken turbans came;
And still the Greek rushed on where the fiery torrent rolled,
Till, like a rising sun shone Xerxes' tent of gold.

They found a royal feast, his midnight banquet there;
And the treasures of the East lay beneath the Doric spear.
Then sat to the repast the bravest of the brave,
That feast must be their last, that spot must be their grave.

Up rose the glorious rank, to Greece one cup poured high,
Then hand in hand they drank, "To immortality!"
Fear on King Xerxes fell, when, like spirits from the tomb,
With shout and trumpet knell, he saw the warriors come.

But down swept all his power, with chariot and with charge;
Down poured the arrow's shower, till sank the Spartan targe.
Thus fought the Greek of old! thus will he fight again.
Shall not the self-same mould bring forth the self-same men?

Desertion of Athens.—"Xerxes, however, having now passed the straits, found nothing capable of opposing his progress in the open country; he therefore directed his march towards Athens, on which he was determined to take signal vengeance.

"Themistocles, seeing little hope of defending the city against the innumerable host of Xerxes, sent to consult the oracle of Apollo, at Delphos. The answer he received was, 'Athens can be saved only by wooden walls.' This he interpreted to mean ships, and acted accordingly. A decree was therefore passed, by which it was ordained, that Athens for awhile should be given up in trust to the gods, and all the inhabitants, whether in freedom or slavery, should go on board the fleet. The young and adventurous set sail for the neighboring island of Salamis; the old, the women and children, took shelter at Troeze'ne, the inhabitants of which generously offered them an asylum. But in this desertion of the city, that which raised the compassion of all was the great number of old men they were obliged to leave in the place, on account of their age and infirmities. Many also voluntarily remained behind, believing that the citadel, which they had fortified with wooden walls, was what the oracle pointed out for general safety. To heighten this scene of distress, the matrons were seen clinging with fond affection to the places where they had so long resided ; the women filled the streets with lamentations; and even the domestic animals seemed to take part in the general concern. It was impossible to see those poor creatures run howling and crying after their masters, who were going on shipboard, without being strongly affected. Amongst these, the faithfulness of a particular dog is recorded, which jumped into the sea, and continued swimming after the vessel that contained his master. The faithful animal landed at Salamis, and died, the moment after, upon the shore."—*Dr. Goldsmith.*

Destruction of Athens.—"The few inhabitants that remained behind retired into the citadel, where, literally interpretating the oracle, they fortified it as well as they could, and patiently awaited the approach of the invader. Nor was it long before they saw him arrive at their gates and summon them to surrender. This, however, they refused to do, or even to listen to any terms he proposed to them. The place was, therefore, taken by assault, all who were found in it were put to the sword, and the citadel reduced to ashes.

" But though the Greeks had been thus obliged to abandon Athens to the fury of the enemy, they were by no means disposed to let them outrun the whole country. They took possession of the Peloponnesus, built a wall across the isthmus that joined it to the continent, and committed the defense of that important post to the brother of Leonidas. In adopting this measure they were unanimous in regarding it as the most prudent that could be embraced, but this was not the case with regard to the operations of the fleet."

Battle of Salamis.—"In spite of opposition Themistocles maintained that it would be the height of folly to abandon so advantageous a post as that of Salamis, where they were now stationed. They were now, he said, in possession of the narrow seas, where the number of the enemy's ships could never avail them. At last his opponents yielded to him, and resolved to await the enemy's fleet at Salamis. Fearful, however, that the confederates might change their mind, Themistocles had recourse to stratagem. He contrived to have it privately intimated to Xerxes, that the Greeks were now assembled at Salamis, preparing for fight, and that it would be an easy matter to attack and destroy them. The artifice succeeded. Xerxes gave order to his fleet to block up Salamis by night, in order to prevent an escape of the Greeks.

"*Aristides*, who commanded a small body of troops at Ægina, no sooner heard of the apparent danger of Themistocles than he ventured in a small boat by night through the whole fleet of the enemy. Upon landing he repaired to the tent of Themistocles, and addressed him in the following manner: 'If we are wise, Themistocles, we shall henceforth lay aside all those frivolous dissensions which have hitherto divided us. One strife, and a noble one it is, now remains to us, which of us shall be most serviceable to our country. It is yours to command as a general, it is mine to obey as a subject, and happy shall I be if my advice can any way contribute to yours and my country's glory.' He then informed him of the fleet's real situation, and warmly exhorted him to give battle without delay. Themistocles felt all that gratitude which so generous and disinterested a conduct deserves, and eager to make a proper return, he immediately let him into his schemes and projects, particularly this last, of suffering himself to be blocked up. After this they exerted their joint influence with the other commanders to persuade them to engage, and accordingly both fleets prepared for battle.

"The Grecian fleet consisted of three hundred and eighty ships, that of the Persians more than a thousand vessels. But whatever advantage they had in numbers and the size of their vessels, they fell infinitely short of the Greeks in naval skill, and in the acquaintance with the seas where they fought. Themistocles, knowing that a periodical wind, which would be favorable, would soon set in, delayed the attack till that time, and this had no sooner arisen than the signal was given for battle, and the Grecian fleet sailed forward in exact order.

"As the Persians now fought under the eye of their sovereign, who beheld the action from a neighboring promonotory, they exerted themselves for some time with great spirit, but their courage abated when they came to a closer engagement. The wind blew directly in their faces, the height and heaviness of their vessels rendered them unwieldy and almost useless, and even the number of their ships only served to embarrass and perplex them in that narrow sea.

"The Ionians, mindful of their Hellenic descent, were far from being anxious for a victory that would enslave the land of their fathers; in the very first onset many of them fled, while others deserted to the Greeks. The Phœnician galleys being thus disordered, and their flanks exposed, dashed against each other, and crowded into a confused mass, deprived of all power of action. The Athenians with skill increased the confusion by forcing fresh hostile ships into the narrow space in which the Phœnicians were entangled. And thus, as the poet Æschylus, who personally shared in the battle, declares, the whole Persian fleet 'was caught and destroyed like fish in a net.'

"Nothing could repair the disorder that had now taken place in the Persian fleet. They fled on all sides; some of them were sunk, and more taken; above two hundred were burnt, and all the rest entirely dispersed.

"Such was the issue of the battle of Salamis, in which the Persians received a more severe blow than any they had hitherto experienced from Greece. Themistocles is said to have been so elated with this victory that he proposed breaking down the bridge over the Hellespont, and thus cutting off the retreat of the enemy; but from this he was dissuaded by Aristides, who represented the danger of reducing so powerful an army to despair."— *Dr. Goldsmith.*

Flight of Xerxes.—"Xerxes, however, seems to have been so apprehensive of this step being taken that after leaving about three hundred thousand of his best troops behind him, under Mardonius, not so much with a view of conquering Greece as in order to prevent a pursuit, he hastened back with the rest to the Hellespont, where, finding the bridge broken down by the waves, he was obliged to pass over in a small boat. His manner of leaving Europe, when compared with his ostentatious entry, rendered his disgrace the more poignant and afflicting."—*Dr. Goldsmith.*

Triumph of Themistocles.—"Nothing could exceed the joy of the Greeks upon the victory they had obtained at Salamis. Themistocles was not only honored by his own countrymen, but was carried in triumph to Sparta. They crowned him with olive, presented him with a rich chariot and conducted him with three hundred horse to the confines of their state.

"When he appeared at the Olympic games (see pages 115, 186, Barnes), before all the states of Greece assembled, the spectators received him with uncommon acclamations. As soon as he appeared the whole assembly rose to do him honor, nobody regarded either the games or the combatants; Themistocles was the only object worthy of their attention. Struck with such flattering honors he could not help exclaiming that he had that day reaped the fruit of all his labors."—*Dr. Goldsmith.*

THE BATTLE OF SALAMIS.

ÆSCHYLUS.

The Persian chief,
Little dreaming of the wiles of Greece
And gods averse, to all the naval leaders
Gave his high charge: "Soon as yon sun shall cease
To dart his radiant beams, and darkening night
Ascends the temple of the sky, arrange
In three divisions your well-ordered ships,
And guard each pass, each outlet of the seas:
Others enring around this rocky isle
Of Salamis. Should Greece escape her fate,

And work her way by secret flight, your heads
Shall answer the neglect." This harsh command
He gave, exulting in his mind, nor knew
What fate designed. With martial discipline
And prompt obedience, snatching a repast,
Each mariner fixed well his ready oar.

Soon as the golden sun was set, and night
Advanced, each, trained to ply the dashing oar,
Assumed his seat; in arms each warrior stood,
Troop cheering troop through all the ships of war.
Each to the appointed station steers his course,
And through the night his naval course each chief
Fixed to secure the passes. Night advanced
But not by secret flight did Greece attempt
To escape. The morn, all beauteous to behold,
Drawn by white steeds, bounds o'er the lightened earth.

At once from every Greek, with glad acclaim,
Burst forth the song of war, whose lofty notes,
The echo of the island rocks returned,
Spreading dismay through Persia's host, thus fallen
From their high hopes; no flight this solemn strain
Portended, but deliberate valor bent
On daring battle; while the trumpet's sound
Kindled the flames of war. But when their oars
(The pæan ended) with impetuous force
Dashed the surrounding surges, instant all
Rushed on in view; in orderly array
The squadron of the right first led; behind
Rode their whole fleet; and now distinct was heard
From every part this voice of exhortation:

"Advance, ye sons of Greece, from thralldom save
Your country—save your wives, your children save,
The temples of your gods, the sacred tomb
Where rest your honored ancestors; this day
The common cause of all demands your valor."
Meanwhile from Persia's hosts the deepening shout
Answered their shout; no time for cold delay;
But ship 'gainst ship its brazen beak impelled.

First to the charge a Grecian galley rushed;
Ill the Phœnician bore the rough attack,
Its sculptured prow all shattered. Each advanced,
Daring an opposite. The deep array
Of Persia at the first sustained the encounter;
But their thronged numbers, in the narrow seas
Confined, want room for action; and, deprived
Of mutual aid, beaks clash with beaks, and each
Breaks all the other's oars; with skill disposed,
The Grecian navy circled them around
In fierce assault; and, rushing from its height,
The inverted vessel sinks.

      The sea no more
Wears its accustomed aspect, with foul wrecks
And blood disfigured; floating carcasses
Roll on the rocky shores; the poor remains
Of the barbaric armament to flight
Ply every oar inglorious; onward rush
The Greeks amid the ruins of the fleet,
As through a shoal of fish caught in the net,
Spreading destruction; the wide ocean o'er
Wailings are heard, and loud laments, till night,
With darkness on her brow, brought grateful truce.
Should I recount each circumstance of woe,
Ten times on my unfinished tale the sun
Would set; for be assured that not one day
Could close the ruin of so vast a host.

"*Mardonius*, having passed the winter in Thessaly, led his forces in the spring into the province of Bœo'tia. Before attacking Attica he sent tempting proposals to the Athenians, offering to rebuild their city, to present them with a considerable sum of money, hoping by this means to detach them from the general interests of Greece. The Athenians rejected with scorn this tempting offer, and at the same time they entreated their allies to join them as speedily as possible, in order to repel a second invasion of Attica. Messenger after messenger was sent to claim the promised aid of Sparta, but all in vain; that state, with the selfishness which characterizes and disgraces its entire history, neglected every summons. They had completed the fortifications of the Corinthian isthmus, and having thus provided, as they believed, for the security of the Peloponnesus, they abandoned northern Greece to the vengeance of the Persians.

"Deserted a second time by the confederates, the Athenians again retired to Salamis, and witnessed from its shores the flames that consumed their houses and temples. Everything that had been spared in the first invasion was destroyed in the second.

"The deputies from Platæa and Megara united with the ambassadors from Athens in reproaching the Spartans for their disgraceful abandonment of the common cause. The Spartans for some time turned a deaf ear to their complaints, until at length the Athenians hinted the probability of their being compelled to accept the offers of Mardonius, and pointed out to the Spartans how vain would be the wall across the isthmus when the Persian fleet, united with that of Athens, would triumphantly sweep the seas, and harass the coast of the Peloponnesus. They immediately resolved to take the field; the different southern states were summoned to send in their contingents, and Pausanias, one of the Macedæmonian kings, was appointed to the command of the combined forces."—*Dr. Goldsmith.*

Battle of Platæa.—"The Grecian army now numbered seventy thousand men. Of these five thousand were

Spartans, attended by thirty-five thousand Helots. The Athenians amounted to eight thousand, and the troops of the allies made up the rest. With this army the Greeks resolved to oppose Mardonius, though at the head of no less than three hundred thousand men.

"The two armies continued in sight of each other for the space of ten days, both equally eager for battle, and yet both afraid to strike the first blow. It was during this interval that a mutiny had nearly arisen in the Grecian army about the post of honor. All parties allowed the Spartans the command of the right wing, but the command of the left was a. position of dispute between Athens and her allies. This dissension might have produced very fatal effects had it not been for the moderation and magnanimity of Aristides, who commanded the Athenians, and who addressed himself to the Spartans and the rest of the confederates in the following manner: 'It is not now a time, my friends, to dispute about the merits of past services, for all boasting is vain in the day of danger. Let it be the brave man's pride to own that it is not the post or station which gives courage, or which can take it away. I head the Athenians. Whatever post you shall assign us we will maintain it, and will endeavor to make our station, wherever we are placed, the post of true honor and military glory. We are come hither not to contend with our friends, but to fight with our enemies; not to boast of our ancestors, but to imitate them. This battle will distinguish the merit of each city, and the lowest sentinel will share with his commander the honor of the day.' This speech determined the council of war in favor of the Athenians, who thereupon were allowed to maintain their former station.

"Meanwhile the Grecians, beginning to be straitened for want of water, resolved to retreat to a place where they might be more plentifully supplied with that necessary article. As their removal was in the night much disorder ensued, and in the morning Mardonius, constructing their retreat into a flight, immediately pursued them, and coming up with them near the little city of Platæa, attacked them with great impetuosity. His ardor, however, was soon checked by the Spartans, who brought up the rear of the Grecian army, and who, throwing themselves into a phalanx, stood impenetrable and immovable against all the assaults of the enemy. At the same time the Athenians, being informed of the attack quickly returned, and, after defeating a body of Greeks in Persian pay, came to the assistance of the Spartans, just as these last had completed the overthrow of the enemy. For Mardonius, enraged at seeing his men give way, rushed into the thickest of the ranks in order to restore the battle, and was killed by a Spartan. Upon this, the whole army betook themselves to flight. A body of forty thousand men fled towards the Hellespont. The rest retreated to the camp, and there endeavored to defend themselves with wooden ramparts, but these being quickly broken down, the Greeks rushed in upon them with irresistible fury, and, eager to rid the country of such terrible invaders, sternly refused them quarter, putting upwards of a hundred thousand of them to the sword."—*Dr. Goldsmith.*

"The whole Persian camp was sacked. Wagon-loads

of silver and gold vessels were to be seen; collars, bracelets, and rich armor and the manger of Xerxes' horses which he had left behind and which was of finely worked brass. A tenth of the spoils was set apart for the temple of Apollo at Delphi." "The same day a victory was gained at Myc'ale, Asia Minor, over the Persian forces in Ionia."—*Miss Yonge and Quackenbos.*

"Thus ended the invasion of Greece by the Persians, nor ever after was an army from Persia seen to cross the Hellespont."—*Dr. Goldsmith.*

THE TOMBS OF PLATÆA.

MRS. HEMANS.

And there they sleep—the men who stood
   In arms before the exulting sun,
And bathed their spears in Persian blood,
   And taught the earth how freedom might be won.

They sleep! The Olympic wreaths are dead,
   The Athenian lyres are hushed and gone;
The Dorian voice of song is fled,—
   Slumber, ye mighty! slumber deeply on!

They sleep, and seems not all around
   As hallowed unto Glory's tomb?
Silence is on the battle-ground,
   The heavens are loaded with a deathless gloom.

And stars are watching on their height,
   But dimly seen through mist and cloud,
And still and solemn is the light
   Which folds the plain as with a glimmering shroud.

And thou, pale night-queen! here thy beams
   Are not as those the shepherd loves;
Nor look they down on shining streams,
   By Naiads haunted, in their laurel groves:

Thou seest no pastoral hamlet sleep
　In shadowy quiet midst its vines;
No temple gleaming from the steep,
　Midst the gray olives on the mountain pines:

But o'er a dim and boundless waste
　Thy rays, e'en like a tomb-lamp's, brood,
Where man's departed steps are traced
　But by his dust amid the solitude.

And be it thus! What slave shall tread
　O'er Freedom's ancient battle-plains?
Let deserts wrap the glorious dead,
　Where their bright land sits weeping o'er her chains:

Here, where their Persian clarion rang,
　And where the Spartan sword flashed high,
And where the pæan strains were sung,
　From year to year swelled on by liberty!

Here should no voice, no sound, be heard,
　Until the bonds of Greece be riven,
Save of the leader's charging word,
　Or the shrill trumpet, pealing up through heaven!

Rest in your silent homes, ye brave!
　No vines festoon your lonely tree!
No harvest o'er your war-folds wave,
　Till rushing winds proclaim,
　　The land is free!

THE ISLES OF GREECE.

BYRON.

The isles of Greece, the isles of Greece!
　Where burning Sappho loved and sung,
Where grew the arts of war and peace,—
　Where Delos rose, and Phœbus sprung!
Eternal summer gilds them yet,
But all, except their sun, is set.

The Scian and the Teian muse,
   The hero's harp, the lover's lute,
Have found the fame your shores refuse;
   Their place of birth alone is mute
To sound which echo further west
Than your sires' "Islands of the Blest."

The mountains look on Marathon—
   And Marathon looks on the sea;
And musing there an hour alone,
   I dreamed that Greece might still be free;
For, standing on the Persians' grave,
I could not deem myself a slave.

A king sat on the rocky brow
   Which looks o'er sea-born Salamis;
And ships, by thousands, lay below,
   And men in nations;—all were his!
He counted them at break of day—
And when the sun set, where were they?

And where are they? and where art thou,
   My country? On thy voiceless shore
The heroic lay is tuneless now—
   The heroic bosom beats no more!
And must thy lyre, so long divine,
Degenerate into hands like mine?

'Tis something, in the dearth of fame,
   Though linked among a fettered race,
To feel at least a patriot's shame,
   Even as I sing, suffuse my face;
For what is left the poet here?
For Greeks a blush,—for Greece a tear.

Must we but weep o'er days more blest?
   Must we but blush?—Our fathers bled.
Earth! render back from out thy breast
   A remnant of our Spartan dead!
Of the three hundred grant but three,
To make a new Thermopylæ!

> What, silent still? and silent all?
>   Ah! no;—the voices of the dead
> Sound like a distant torrent's fall,
>   And answer, "Let one living head,
> But one arise,—we come, we come!"
> 'Tis but the living who are dumb.

Athenian Supremacy.—Athens was quickly rebuilt and its walls fortified and extended, with a view to greater security in the future. This excited the jealousy of the Lacedæmonians, who sent ambassadors to dissuade them from the undertaking. Themistocles skillfully delayed treating with them until the works were completed and then sent back a defiant answer.

This spirited conduct ended the trouble for a time, and instead of drawing their swords against each other they fitted out a powerful fleet to establish the Grecian dominion on the islands and shores of the Ægean. Pausanias commanded the Spartans; the Athenians were conducted by Aristides, and Cimon, the son of Miltiades.

Byzantium was taken and plundered. A great number of prisoners were captured, many of whom were of the richest and noblest families of Persia. "But whatever the Greeks gained upon this occasion in fame and authority, they lost in purity and simplicity of their manners. The deluge of wealth poured in upon them from this quarter naturally tended to corrupt their minds; and from this time forward neither the magistrates nor the people valued themselves, as formerly, on their personal merit, but merely on account of their riches and possessions."—*Dr. Goldsmith.*

Fate of Pausanias.—The Athenians were not so soon demoralized by this prosperity, but it proved the ruin of

Pausanias, who was led by his ambitious schemes to play the part of a cowardly traitor to his country. "He offered to deliver up Sparta, and even all of Greece, to Xerxes, provided that prince would give him his daughter in marriage." The Spartan magistrates became acquainted with his designs and ordered his arrest. "He took refuge in the temple of Minerva, where the sanctity of the place prevented him from being dragged forth. The people blocked up the entrance with stones, and tearing off the roof, left him to die of cold and hunger. Thus perished the man who had led on the troops of Greece to victory in the battle of Plataea."—*Dr. Goldsmith.*

Themistocles Exiled.—The fate of Pausanias soon after involved that of Themistocles. He was thought to have favored the designs of Pausanias, a crime of which it afterward appeared he was altogether guiltless. The fact that he gained great wealth while in office influenced his countrymen to accuse him of obtaining it by illegitimate means. He also built near his house a temple in honor of Diana, bearing the inscription, "To Diana, the goddess of good counsel," intimating thereby that he had given the best counsel, not only to the Athenians but to all Greece. For this presumption he had been banished by the Athenians, but now the Spartans, his old enemies, accused him of being an accomplice of Pausanias, and the Athenians, who had been envious of his former popularity, joined in the charge against him. The people were so engraged that they clamored for his death. Officers were sent to seize him and bring him for trial before a counsel of Greeks; but having timely notice of it he fled.

After various wandering, he at last reached Sardis, and prostrating hinself before the Persian king, boldly declared his name, his country and his misfortunes. "I have done my ungrateful country services more than once," said he, "and I am now come to offer those services to you. My life is in your hands; you may now exert your clemency or display your vengeance. By the former you will preserve a faithful suppliant, by the latter you will destroy the greatest enemy of Greece."

The king was highly pleased with his eloquence and boldness. His admiration for Themistocles led him to confer the most distinguished honors upon him, and gave him the revenues of three cities for the support of himself and family who had followed him into exile.

But nothing could erase from the breast of Themistocles the love he entertained for his country, though the ingratitude of his countrymen had hardened his heart for awhile. "When Artaxerxes, therefore, proposed fitting out an expedition against Athens, and intrusting the command of it Themistocles, that patriot, rather than carry arms against the place of his nativity, put an end to his own life by poison."—*Dr. Goldsmith.*

Rule of Aristides.—In the meantime, Aristides continued every day to win a larger share of the esteem and veneration of his countrymen by his integrity and love of justice. So great was his character in this respect that he was considered the only person in the country to be intrusted with the public treasure. Implicit confidence was placed in him, for while his friends rolled in luxury and affluence, he remained in poverty. Aristides died (375 B. C.) greatly honored, though he was so poor that he did not have enough money to pay his funeral expenses, but a monument was raised to him by the state, and his family were supported by pensions. Only one other Athenian name was held to be as pure and noble as that of Aristides.

Cimon.—"The first man who began to make a figure at Athens after the death of Themistocles and Aristides was Ci'mon, the son of Milti'ades. In his earlier years he had led a very dissolute life; but Aristi'des, perceiving in him, amidst all his dissipation, the seeds of many great and good qualities, advised him to change his conduct, and to raise his mind from the pursuit of low and ignoble pleasures to the ambition of directing the affairs of the state. He did so, and in a short time, became equal to his father in courage, to Themistocles in sagacity, and not much inferior to his instructor himself in integrity."—*Dr. Goldsmith.*

Under the leadership of Cimon the Greeks achieved many brilliant successes over the Persians, and, in 450 B. C., concluded a treaty, with Artaxerxes I, on terms the most honorable to Greece. "It was stipulated that all the Greek cities in Asia should be free, and that no Persian army should come within three days' march of the coast, and that no Persian vessel should set sail on the Ægean sea. Such was the conclusion of this memorable war, which, without interruption, had lasted for half a century. The same magnanimous republic that first dared to brave the resentment of the greatest empire of the world had the honor of prescribing the condition of peace."

Jealousy of the Greeks.—"The war between Greece and Persia had checked without destroying the mutual jealousies between the leading states, and now Sparta, Argos, and Thebes began to look with envy on the glory that Athens had obtained by her immortal victories. The Spartans in particular were enraged with themselves for having withdrawn so early from a war so productive of fame and profit to their rivals. They were still more indignant because the maritime states had chosen Athens as their guardian and their head. Twenty years before the peace with Persia the Spartans had determined to make war on the Athenians, but unexpected calamities engaged their attention at home and brought their state to the very brink of destruction."—*Dr. Goldsmith.*

Revolt of the Helots.—"Laconia was laid waste by one of the most dreadful earthquakes recorded in history (469 B. C.). The city of Sparta was tumbled into ruins, and twenty thousand of the inhabitants were destroyed. The Helots, believing that the moment for recovering their liberty was arrived, took possession of a strong fortress and spread terror through all Laconia. This revolt compelled the Spartans, much against their will, to solicit the assistance of the Athenians, who were considered the most skillful of all the Greeks in conducting sieges. Their request was granted, but the strength of the besieged baffled their united efforts, and the auxiliaries were sent home. This war continued ten years, and must have greatly exhausted the Spartan state, since at its conclusion very favorable terms were granted to the insurgents. It was stipulated that they should be allowed to depart with their wives, children and property, unmolested from the Peloponnesus. The Athenians received the exiles with great kindness, and bestowed on them the city Naupactus, a seaport on the Crissean gulf. The fugitives repaid the generosity of Athens by the most devoted attachment, nor had that city a more faithful ally than Naupactus during the subsequent wars."—*Dr. Goldsmith.*

Age of Pericles.—" Cimon, during his lifetime, used every exertion to restore and preserve peace between Athens and Sparta; he was at the head of the nobility, whose assistance, added to his own military glory, made him at first the most influential man in the state. (See Barnes, page 136.) But he soon met with a formidable rival in *Pericles,* the greatest statesman of antiquity. Though descended from an illustrious family, he placed himself at the head of the popular party, and, by his superior eloquence, wielded at will that fierce democracy. Though his military fame did not equal that of Cimon, he was second only to that illustrious general in the art of war; but in political skill Pericles was unequalled, and even had sufficient influence to procure the temporary banishment of his rival."—*Dr. Goldsmith.*

His aim was to make Athens the seat of art and refinement and procure for her the supremacy of Greece. As the leader of the democracy he sought to make the people all powerful in Athens. This he accomplished by introducing the custom of military pay, by attaching salaries to all civil offices so that the poorest citizen might aspire to the highest magistracy. In this manner the power of the court of Areopagus, the stronghold of aristocracy, was broken. In order that the people might become qualified to exert their influence in government he secured the payment of citizens who served on the jury or attended the meetings of the popular assembly. To gain their favor as well as to promote their education free tickets to the theaters and other places of amusement were supplied. Never before had any people enjoyed such perfect political liberty nor obtained so intimate a knowledge of public affairs.

"Athens, thus ruled, became a great imperial city, extending protection to the less powerful states and exacting from them in return obedience and tribute. Her fleet became mistress of the eastern Mediterranean; wealth flowed into her treasury, and most of the islands of the Ægean, with many colonies and conquered territories, acknowledged her sway."—*Quackenbos.*

The riches that Pericles obtained were faithfully laid out in increasing the navy and ornamenting the city of Athens. His enemies accused him of appropriating money from the common treasury to adorn Athens "as a vain woman decks herself out with jewels." Pericles replied that the money was contributed by the league for protection against the Persians, "and so long as the Athenians kept the enemy at a distance they had a right to use the money as they pleased." It was his design that the arts and crafts at home should be employed and have their share of the public moneys as well as those maintained in the armaments abroad.

The summit of the Acropolis, a level plain eight hundred feet in length and nearly four hundred in breadth, was chosen as the site for those masterpieces of architecture which were erected by Pericles and other statesmen to be the glory of their own age and the admiration of posterity. Here were erected the unrivaled Parthenon, the entrance to the citadel or Propylæa, the treasury, and the courts. At the foot of the Acropolis were the Odeum, where musical contests were celebrated, and the theater of Bacchus, where the great tragedies were acted in honor of that deity. (See page 165, Barnes.)

The lower city itself contained no structures worthy of mention, since the Athenians were forbidden by law to use any display in the construction of their own private dwellings. The Athenian Agora or market-place was surrounded by porticos ornamented by busts and statues, by such paintings as the burning of Troy and the battle of Marathon, and by moral sentences written for the instruction of the people. It was under the shade of one of these porticos that Zeno taught his disciples, whence his followers were called *Stoics*, from a Greek word (*stoa'*), signifying a porch.

The only temple in the lower city was the temple of Theseus, a beautiful structure. It was erected in memory of Theseus, who had ever been the protector of the distressed, and therefore had the privilege of being a sanctuary for slaves and all men of the lower ranks who dreaded persecution.

As a part of his maritime policy Pericles built the Long Walls connecting Athens with its port Piræus. "The Long Walls were each between four and five miles in length and sixty feet high. They were defended by numerous towers, which, when Athens became crowded, were used as shops and private dwellings. The walls were employed as highways, the top being wide enough to allow two chariots to pass conveniently. The foundation of the northern wall now forms in part the road-bed of the railroad running from Piræus to Athens." "With her communication at sea thus secured, and with a powerful army at her command, Athens could bid defiance to her foes on sea and land."—*Dr. Goldsmith.*

The *Age of Pericles,* though it embraced less than the lifetime of a single generation, gave birth to more great men—poets, artists, statesmen and philosophers—than all the world besides has produced in any period of equal length. Yet among all these great names that of Pericles ranks pre-eminent, for his commanding statesmanship, his persuasive eloquence, and almost universal genius.

Strength and Weakness of the Athenian Empire.— Athens had become the most powerful naval state in the world, but she had reached the summit of her greatness. The Persian wars had checked the power of Persia. Rome had not yet risen to prominence, and Carthage was only able to contend with the Greek cities of Sicily. Indisputably the Hellenes were at this moment the predominant race of the world, and Athens was the real head of Hellas. Never before had there been such a union of the material and intellectual elements of civilization at the seat of empire. " Literature and art had been carried to the utmost perfection possible to human genius," yet the Athenian empire rested upon a foundation of sand. The spirit of freedom lived not only in Athens but was smouldering in all her subject cities. The so-called confederates were the slaves of Athens. "To her they paid tribute. To her courts they were dragged for trial." She was the hateful tyrant whose yoke they were impatient to throw off. If Athens had but known how to retain her rivals as co-workers and fellow-countrymen what might not have been the future of the Hellenes!

Another deep-rooted evil had been planted in the bosom of the democracy itself. Pericles himself had sown the seed. A system which provides payment for the smallest public service and establishes the wholesale distribution of public gifts can not fail to produce a fawning, improvident, idle people.

The results of this erroneous policy soon became evident in the struggle between Athens and Sparta called the Peloponnesian war.—*Adapted from Myers.*

GREEK ART.

First Grecian Temples.—"In the earliest times the Greeks had no temples save the forests. The statues of the gods were first placed beneath the shelter of a tree or within its hollow trunk. After a time a building rudely constructed of the trunks of trees, and shaped like the habitations of men, marked the first step in advance. Then stone took the place of the wooden frame. With the introduction of a durable material the artist was encouraged to spend more care and labor on his work. Thus architecture began to make rapid strides, and by the century following the age of Solon at Athens, there were many beautiful temples in different parts of the Hellenic world."—*Myers.*

The Greek Sense of Beauty.—"The Greeks were artists by nature. They possessed an organism that was most exquisitely sensitive to impressions of the beautiful. As it has been expressed, ugliness gave them pain like a blow. Everything they made, from the shrines of their gods to the meanest utensils of domestic use, was beautiful. Beauty they placed next to holiness; indeed they almost, or quite, made beauty and moral right the same thing. It is said that it was noted by the Greek as something strange and exceptional that Socrates was good, notwithstanding he was ugly in feature.

"The first maxim in Greek art, as well as morality, was: 'Nothing in excess.' The Greek eye was offended at any lack of symmetry or proportion in an object. The proportions of the Greek temple are perfect. Clearness of outline was another requirement of Greek taste. It is possible that nature itself taught the Greeks these first principles of art. Nature in Greece never goes to extremes. The Grecian mountains and islands are never over large. The climate is never excessively cold nor oppressively hot. And Nature here seems to abhor vagueness. The singular transparency of the atmosphere lends a remarkable clearness of outline to every object. The Parthenon seems modeled after the hills that lie with such absolute clearness of form against the Attic sky."—*Myers.*

FOREST HYMN.

BRYANT.

The groves were God's first temples. Ere man learned
To hew the shaft, and lay the architrave,
And spread the roof above them—ere he framed
The lofty vault, to gather and roll back
The sound of anthems; in the darkling wood,
Amidst the cool and silence, he knelt down
And offered to the Mightiest, solemn thanks
And supplication. For his simple heart
Might not resist the sacred influences,
Which, from the stilly twilight of the place,
And from the gray old trunks that high in heaven
Mingled their mossy boughs, and from the sound
Of the invisible breath that swayed at once
All their green tops, stole over him, and bowed
His spirit with the thought of boundless power
And inaccessible majesty. Ah, why
Should we, in the world's riper years, neglect
God's ancient sanctuaries, and adore
Only among the crowd, and under roofs
That our frail hands have raised? Let me, at least
Here, in the shadow of this aged wood,
Offer one hymn—thrice happy, if it find
Acceptance in his ear.

Orders of Architecture.—"Before speaking of the most noted temples of Hellas, we must first name the three styles or orders of Grecian architecture. These are the Doric, the Ionic, and the Corinthian. They are distinguished from one another chiefly by differences in the proportions and ornamentation of the column.

"The Doric column is without a base, and has a simple and massive capital. The prototype of this order may be seen at Beni Hassan, in Egypt. At first the Doric temples of the Greeks were almost as massive as the Egyptian temples, but later they became more refined.

"The Ionic column is characterized by the spiral volutes of the capital. This form was borrowed from the Assyrians, and was principally employed by the Ionians, whence its name.

"The Corinthian order is distinguished by its rich capital, formed of acanthus leaves. This type is made up of Egyptian, Assyrian and Grecian elements. The bell shape of the capital is in imitation of the Egyptian style. The addition of the acanthus leaves is said to have been suggested to the artist by the pretty effect of a basket surrounded by the leaves of an acanthus plant, upon which it had accidentally fallen. This order was not much employed in Greece before the time of Alexander the great."—*Myers*.

The Parthenon.—The finest specimen of Greek architecture is the Parthenon, or temple of Pallas Athena, on the Acropolis. It was built in the Doric order of purest Pentelic marble, embellished by the sculptures of Phidias, and by bright colorings. The color is not seen now except in odd fragments dug from the ground, but all is a beautiful gold brown transformed by the Attic dust of ages. (See page 147, Mahaffy.) The renown of this masterpiece of architecture is not due to its vastness but to its marvelous symmetry, and the perfection of even the invisible parts. This extraordinary finish, which can only be seen from the roof, or by opening a wall, proves that the builders wrought for the glory of their god, and not for the praise of man. Longfellow has skillfully woven this thought into his poem of "The Builders:"

> "In the elder days of art
> Builders wrought with greatest care
> Each minute and unseen part,
> For the gods are everywhere."
>
> (Page 97, Indiana Fifth Reader.)

"The temple contained three statues of Minerva or Pallas Athena, one of olive wood so ancient that it was said to have fallen from heaven, one of marble and one of gold and ivory, the work of Phidias, and deemed, next to his statue of the Olympic Jupiter, the greatest triumph of sculpture."—*Dr. Goldsmith.* (See page 181, Barnes.)

The wonderful frieze which ornamented the temple was also the work of Phidias. It represented a procession of youths in an Athenian festival, which was celebrated every four years in honor of the patron goddess of Athens.

"After standing for more than two thousand years as a pagan temple, a Christian church and a Mohammedan mosque, it finally was made to serve as a Turkish powder magazine in a war with the Venetians in 1687. During the progress of this contest a bomb fired the magazine, and more than half of this masterpiece of ancient art was shivered into fragments. The front is still quite perfect, and is the most prominent feature of the Acropolis at the present day. The larger part of the frieze is now in the British museum, the Parthenon having been despoiled of its coronal of sculptures by Lord Elgin."—*Myers*.

Temple of Diana.—"The temple of Diana at Ephesus was one of the oldest, as well as one of the most famous, of the sacred edifices of the Greeks. Crœsus gave liberally of his wealth to ornament the shrine. It was known far and wide as one of the Seven Wonders of the World. Alexander placed within the shrine his own portrait, worth $30,000. The value of the gifts to the temple was beyond all calculation; kings and states vied with one another in splendid donations. Painters and sculptors were eager to have their masterpieces assigned a place within its walls, so that it became a great national gallery of paintings and statuary. The Grecian temples were, in a certain sense, banks of deposit. They contained special chambers or vaults for the safe-keeping of valuables."—*Myers*.

"**Temple at Olympia** was built of porous stone, the roof being tiled with Pentelic marble. It stood on the banks of the Alpheus, in a sacred grove of plane and olive trees. The statue of Jupiter, by Phidias, was so superstitiously venerated that not to have seen it was considered a real calamity. The statue, sixty feet high, was seated on an elaborately sculptured throne of cedar, inlaid with gold, ivory, ebony and precious stones; like the statue of Athena in the Parthenon, the face, feet and body were of ivory; the eyes were brilliant jewels and the hair and beard pure gold. The drapery was beaten gold, enameled with flowers. One hand grasped a scepter, composed of precious metals and surmounted by an eagle; in the other, like Athena, he held a golden statue of victory. The statue was so high, in proportion to the building, that the Greeks were wont to say that 'if the god should attempt to rise he would burst open the roof.' The effect of its great size was to impress the beholder with the pent-up power and majesty of the greatest of the gods. A copy of the head of this statue is in the Vatican. The statue itself, removed to Constantinople by the Emperor Theodosius I, was lost in the disastrous fire (A. D. 475) which destroyed the library in that city. At the same time perished the Venus of Cnidos by Praxiteles, which the ancients ranked next to the Phidian Zeus and Athena."—*Myers*.

DECLINE OF GREECE.

"The Peloponnesian Wars (431-404 B. C.), is the name given to that long struggle between the two great representatives of aristocracy and democracy—Sparta and Athens." A league including the most powerful states of continental Greece was formed to humble the power of the Athenians. "A slight cause sufficed to provoke hostilities." A dispute having arisen between Corinth and one of her island colonies—Cocyra, Athens favored the latter, and sent a fleet against the Corinthians. "Corinth complained to the Peloponnersian alliance at Sparta. Other states brought charges against Athens and finally war was declared.

"A Spartan army was soon overrunning Attica, but Pericles gathered the people within the walls of Athens and confined himself to naval operations on the Peloponnesian coasts. He would not risk an engagement with the Spartans, replying to those who demanded to be led against the enemy, 'Trees cut down may shoot again, but men are not to be replaced.'

"The crowded condition of the city brought on a pestilence, which carried off the inhabitants by thousands, and among them Pericles himself (429 B. C.) His death left Athens in the hands of demagogues, who were ready to sacrifice the public interests to their own selfish purposes." Still Athens triumphed for a while.—*Quackenbos*.

At the end of twenty-seven years of almost constant warfare, 404 B. C., the proud city was doomed. "Her treasury was empty, her allies had forsaken her, Persian gold lent weight to the Lacedæmonian sword. Sparta having captured the Athenian squadron, blockaded the city itself. Famine threatened, and the imperial city surrendered 404 B. C. Her fortifications were destroyed and the Long Walls were demolished amid the insulting triumphs of music.

Thus ended the supremacy of Athens as a naval power, but she still remained "mistress of Greece in art and literature."

Oppressive Rule of Sparta.—Sparta had assumed the character of Liberator of Greece, but the cities found that they had simply exchanged masters. "Instead, however, of the rule of a polished state they now must submit to the harsh, rapacious laws of Sparta."

"At Athens the democratic constitution was abolished and the government placed in the hands of thirty aristocrats called the Thirty Tyrants." These men ruled with such notorious injustice and cruelty that their terror was quickly ended and the democracy re-established, 403 B. C.—*Quackenbos*.

Socrates.—"The unjust doom of the philosopher Socrates darkens the next page of Athenian history. He was the most enlightened of heathen sages, taught the immortality of the soul, and looked above the absurd

mythology of his native land for something higher and purer to believe. Charged with setting up new deities and corrupting the young, he was sentenced to drink the fatal hemlock. In vain his friends provided means of escape and besought him to fly. He firmly refused to violate the laws, and calmly drained the cup of poison in the midst of his weeping associates."—*Quackenbos.*
(Page 175, Barnes; chapter xxiii, Miss Yonge's Y. Folks' H.)

Xenophon and *Plato* were two of his distinguished disciples. (See Retreat of the Ten Thousand, chapter xxii, Miss Yonge; Guerber's Greek Stories.)

Theban Rule.—(See Guerber and Miss Yonge.) When the oppressive rule of Sparta was at its height there arose in Thebes a great general Epaminondas, who made the Theban army the best in all Greece. "The famous victory of Leuctra (371 B. C.), in which four thousand Lacedæmonians, together with their king, were slain, secured for Thebes the sovereignty of Greece." On this famous field the Spartans were beaten for the first time in history. Epaminondas drew up his troops in a column fifty men deep, with which he dashed at the middle of the Spartan army, which was only three lines deep. The plan succeeded perfectly. The Spartan king was carried dying from the field, and Epaminondas had won the most difficult victory ever won by a Greek. So far from being uplifted by it, he only replied that his greatest pleasure was in thinking how it would gratify his father and mother. (See page 147, Barnes.)

When the defeat became known in Sparta the fathers

and relations of those who had fallen in battle went to the temples to thank the gods and congratulate each other upon their glory and good fortune, whilst the relations of those who had escaped were overwhelmed with grief and affliction.

The law of the Spartans condemned the survivors of a defeat to be degraded from all honor. They were to appear publicly in mean, dirty and patched garments, and to go half shaved, and whoever met them in the streets might insult and beat them without their daring to make any resistance. On this occasion such numbers had incurred the penalties of the law, many of whom were of the best families, that they feared the execution of it might excite some public commotion. The king was urged to abolish the law, but not wishing to do that, he made a public declaration that the law should lie dormant for that single day, and thus saved the citizens from infamy.

Epaminondas, the victorious general of the Thebans, now sought to restore the freedom of the enslaved states of Greece and form a union against the further tyranny of Sparta. Athens at first aided him, and then, jealous of his success, sided with the Lacedæmons.

A battle was fought at Mantinea, 362 B. C., and in the very moment of victory, Epaminondas fell pierced by a javalin. "The weapon remained in his breast, nor would his friends remove it, knowing that he would die the instant it was withdrawn. The Theban chief bore the agony of his wound until assured that his triumph was complete. 'Then, all is well,' he said, and drawing out the fatal spear-head, breathed his last. In answer

to the sorrowing spectators who lamented that so great a man should die childless Epaminondas exclaimed, 'I leave you two fair daughters—Leuctra and Mantinea.'"
—*Adapted from Goldsmith.*

" Epaminondas was a pure, unselfish patriot, a refined, moral, and generous citizen. Cicero calls him the greatest man Greece ever produced.

"The battle of Mantinea, which all Greece watched in suspense, was indecisive in its results. Thebes, the head of Greece while Epaminondas lived, now sank to her former level. The glory of Hellas had departed. Exhausted by these struggles, and torn by the social and sacred wars that followed, she rapidly declined. Her ruin was due to the mutual jealousies of the several states. Disunited and demoralized Greece at last lay prostrate and ready for the spoiler—and in Philip, of Macedon, the spoiler was soon to appear."—*Quackenbos.*

THE AGES.

BRYANT.

. . . .

And virtue can not dwell with slaves, nor reign
   O'er those who cower to take a tyrant's yoke:
She left the down-trod nations in disdain,
   And flew to Greece, when liberty awoke,
New-born, amid those beautiful vales, and broke
   Scepter and chain with her fair, youthful hands,
As the rock shivers in the thunder-stroke.
   And lo! in full-grown strength, an empire stands
Of leagued and rival states, the wonder of the lands.

O Greece, thy flourishing cities were a spoil
  Unto each other; thy hard hand oppressed
And crushed the helpless; thou didst make thy soil
  Drunk with the blood of those that loved thee best;
And thou didst drive, from thy unnatural breast,
  Thy just and brave to die in distant climes;
Earth shuddered at thy deeds, and sighed for rest
  From thine abominations; after times
That yet shall read thy tale, will tremble at thy crimes.

Yet there was that within thee which has saved
  Thy glory and redeemed thy blotted name;
The story of thy better deeds, engraved
  On fame's unmoldering pillar, puts to shame
Our chiller virtue; the high art to tame
  The whirlwind of the passions was thine own;
And the pure ray that from thy bosom came,
  Far over many a land and age has shone,
And mingles with the light that beams from God's own throne.

. . . .

THE MACEDONIAN EMPIRE.

Macedonia was a mountainous country north of Thessaly. Its early history is uncertain, but though the Macedonians themselves spoke a rude language and were deemed by the Greeks as almost barbarians, their kings claimed to have descended from Hercules, and were permitted to take part in the Olympic games.

Philip of Macedon.—During the period of Theban supremacy in Greece there were rival competitors who claimed the throne of Macedonia and the country was distracted by civil wars. The Thebans sent an army into Macedonia to support the cause of the rightful heirs, and Philip, then a boy, was sent as a hostage to Thebes.

At the death of his brother, Philip became king. He was twenty-four years of age and had received a considerable part of his education under Epaminondas at Thebes. "There he became acquainted with the military system of the Thebans, studied the Greek character, and acquired that diplomacy which afterward gained him many a bloodless victory."

Formation of Phalanx.—His first care in taking up the reins of government was to gain the affections of his people and to raise their spirits, for they had become very much disheartened by heavy losses in battle. "His next step was to train and exercise them and reform their discipline." "Philip improved on the Theban tactics by instituting the Macedonian phalanx, a body of 16,000 heavily armed foot soldiers." Each soldier carried a shield and a spear twenty-four feet long. When they advanced, they were taught to lock their shields together, so as to form a wall, and they stood in ranks, one behind the other, so that the front row had four spear points projecting before them. (See page 149, Barnes.)

Philip also formed a guard of honor at his court composed of the sons of the nobles. Thus there grew up in his service a trusty band of followers who were his comrades, his friends, and his officers.

"In less than two years he triumphed over the enemies in his own kingdom and was ready to enlarge its boundaries. He availed himself of the quarrels of the Greeks to seize their colonial cities, conquered Thessaly, and took possession of the rich gold mines of Thrace. Through the folly of the Thebans he was invited to interfere in the so-called sacred war, and as a victor he was rewarded by a seat in the Am-phic-ty-on'-ic Council." (See page 115, Barnes.)

Thus he gained a footing which forwarded his scheme for subjugating the entire peninsula.

"The Athenians, meanwhile, the only people that might have checked Philip's career, were cajoled by the crafty king and remained inactive. There was one at Athens, however, that saw through Philip's wiles—the eloquent Demosthenes, who, for years, struggled nobly against him in defense of Grecian liberty."—*Compiled from Goldsmith and Quackenbos.* (See page 262, Miss Yonge.)

Chærone'a.—Roused at last by the burning eloquence of Demosthenes, Athens and Thebes made a desperate stand at Chæronea, in Bœotia, against the Macedonian monarch, who had passed Thermopylœ and was occupying the cities of Greece. But the charge of the phalanx proved irresistible. The allies were totally defeated; and while Demosthenes, brave as he had been in words, fled from the field, the Sacred Band of Epaminondas was cut down to a man, thus gloriously dying with the independence of Hellas, 338 B. C. Philip thus became master of Greece, and, by a council of all the states except Sparta, was appointed to lead their united forces against Persia. But before the preparations for the expedition were completed, Philip met his death by the dagger of an assassin when celebrating his daughter's nuptials, 336 B. C.

(See anecdotes of Philip: Barnes, Miss Yonge, Guerber.)

Alexander the Great.—Philip's son, known in history

as Alexander the Great, succeeded to the throne when he was but twenty years old. Certain noted events transpiring on the day of his birth, namely, the victory gained by Philip's chief general, and the winning of the prize at the Olympic games, also the burning the temple of Diana at Ephesus, were considered, in that superstitious age, premonitions of future greatness.

In order to insure the accomplishment of these predictions, Philip obtained for his son the best masters, and at the age of fifteen placed him under the care of Aristotle, pupil of Plato, and one of the greatest and best of philosophers. Alexander was an apt and attentive student, and easily mastered not only sciences but polite literature also. "He was greatly delighted with Homer's Iliad, and, it is thought, modeled himself upon the warlike heroes of that poem." The character of Achilles, said to have been his own ancestor, he considered most worthy of his imitation.

"In early life Alexander gave proof of his military genius. He excelled in all manly sports, and when very young subdued a fiery steed called Buceph'alus, or Bullhead, because of a white mark like a bull's face on its forehead." The horse was so strong and restive that nobody could manage it, and Philip was sending it away, when Alexander begged leave to try. "First he turned his head to the sun, having perceived that its antics were caused by fear of its own shadow; then stroking and caressing it as he held the reins, he gently dropped his fluttering mantle and leaped on its back, sitting firm through all its leaps and bounds, but using neither whip nor spur nor angry voice, till at last the creature was brought to perfect obedience. This gentle courage and firmness so delighted Philip that he embraced the boy with tears of joy, and gave him the horse. Bucephalus afterwards carried his master through many campaigns, but never allowed any other to mount him."—*Miss Yonge.*

"At an early age Alexander was introduced by his father into public life. He received the Persian ambassadors when not quite sixteen, and astonished them by his pertinent inquiries respecting the political condition and revenues of Persia. Soon after he was appointed regent of Macedon, while his father was besieging Byzantium. Two years after he commanded the left wing of the Macedonian army at the battle of Chærone'a, and cut down the sacred Theban band."—*Goldsmith.*

"As soon as Alexander was proclaimed king he marched to Corinth, and the assembled states of Greece were again compelled to recognize the supremacy of Macedon, while they made him commander-in-chief of the Grecian forces in the projected enterprise against the Persians."

Before leaving for Persia, however, he determined to put his own country into a secure condition; so he turned northward to subdue the wild tribes in Thrace. He was gone four months, "and the Thebans, misled by a false report of the young prince's death, rebelled. Suddenly Alexander appeared before the city, carried it by storm, and razed it to the ground, sparing only the house of the poet Pindar. The Thebans that survived were sold into slavery, and all Greece, terror-stricken by this fearful example, abjectly submitted to the conqueror."—*Quackenbos*. (Story of Diogenes, page 275, Miss Yonge.)

Invasion of Persia.—"Being desirous to consult the oracle at Delphi as to his expedition into Asia, Alexander visited the temple of Apollo. But as it was an unlucky day, the priestess refused to approach the shrine. The king grasped her arm and drew her forward. 'Ah! my son,' said she, 'you are irresistible.' 'Enough,' exclaimed Alexander, 'I desire no other response.'

"Having completed his preparations and made his father's councilor governor of Macedon in his absence, Alexander started for the East, 334 B. C." With the small army of but 30,000 foot and 5,000 cavalry, he was hoping to subdue a country "that stretched from the Ægean to Scythia and from the Euxine to the African deserts. Such was his liberality in gifts before he went away, that when he was asked what he had left for himself, he answered, 'my hopes.' His intentions were not merely to conquer that great world, but to tame it, bring it into order, and teach the men there the wisdom and free spirit of the great world; for he had learned from Aristotle that to make men true, brave, virtuous and free was the way to be god-like. It was in his favor that the direct line of Persian kings had failed and that there had been wars and factions all through the last reign."—*Miss Yonge.*

Alexander Crosses the Hellespont.—Alexander steered his own vessel across the Hellespont and was the first to leap ashore. He first visited the plain of Troy and all the scenes described in the Iliad and then offered sacrifices at the mound, said to be the tomb of Achilles.

The Persian forces gave battle to the Greeks on the banks of the river *Granicus*, a stream flowing into the Euxine. "Alexander wore a white plume in his helmit so that all might know him. It was a grand victory, though not without much hard fighting. Alexander was once in great danger, but was saved by Clitus, the son of his nurse. The Persian army was so entirely routed that no army was left in Asia Minor, and the satrap killed himself in despair. Alexander forbade his troops to plunder the country, telling them that it was his own, and that the people were as much his subjects as they were. Sardis and Ephesus fell into his hands without a blow; and to assist in rebuilding the great temple of Diana, he granted all the tribute hitherto paid to the great king."—*Miss Yonge.*

"On the approach of winter, leave of absence was given to the Macedonians to visit their families; and they on their return spread the fame of their victories through all Greece. Alexander did not spend the winter in idleness; he extended his conquest over several minor provinces, arranged the government of those already subdued, and removed his headquarters to Gordium, a central city of Asia Minor."

"Gordium was celebrated as the residence of king Midas, and the line of Phrygian kings descended from him." Here he was shown the famous Gordian knots, which, it was said, no one could untie except the one destined to be the conqueror of Asia. "How the king effected his purpose is uncertain. Some say that he cut the knot with his sword, others, that he really solved the difficulty; certain it is they believed him to have fulfilled the conditions of the oracle, and to be consequently the destined lord of Asia."—*Dr. Goldsmith.*

"In the spring he dashed down through the Taurus mountains, to take possession of the city of Tarsus." By this rapid march Memnon, the Persian general, was prevented from carrying out his plan for devastating the country. "The fatigue of the march and the heat of the weather overpowered the young king; hoping to refresh himself, he imprudently plunged into the cold waters of the Cnidus, a mountain stream, and was instantaneously seized with violent fever, which threatened fatal consequences. While suffering under this disease, Alexander exhibited a noble example of intrepid courage and generous confidence. He received a letter, denouncing his physician Philip as a traitor, who had been bribed to take him off by poison, at the very moment that the physician stood by his bedside with the medicinal draught. The king, presenting the letter to Phillip, unhesitatingly drank off the portion; his confidence was amply repaid, for the medicine brought about a favorable change, and in a short time he was restored to his anxious army."—*Dr. Goldsmith.*

Battle of Issus.—Darius, the Persian king, was now advancing with a large army, "in which was a band of Spartans, who hated the Persians less than they did the Macedonians. The Persian march was a splendid sight. The army never marched until sunrise, when silver altars bearing the sacred fire were carried first, attended by a band of youths, one for each day in the year; then followed the chariot of the sun drawn by white horses, after which came a horse consecrated to the sun, and led by white-robed attendants. "The king himself sat in a high, richly adorned chariot, wearing a purple mantle, encrusted with precious stones and encompassed with his immortal band, in robes adorned with gold, and carrying silver-handled lances. In covered chariots were his mother, his wives and children, their baggage occupying six hundred mules and three hundred camels, all protected by so enormous an army every one thought the Macedonians must be crushed."—*Miss Yonge.*

Nevertheless Alexander attacked them at Issus and gained a great victory. "When Darius saw his immortals giving way he fled from the field with so much rapidity that his chariot, bow, and royal mantle fell into the hands of the victors." His army, even to the cavalry, imitated his example. "The Persian camp, with all its enormous wealth, was the immediate result of the victory. Among the captives were the mother, queen, and daughters of Darius, whom Alexander treated with the greatest kindness and generosity."—*Dr. Goldsmith.*

"He showed the mother of Darius special kindness and respect, even more than she had ever received from her own kindred. He never grieved her but once, and that was when he showed her a robe spun, woven, and worked by his mother and sisters for himself, and offered to have her grandchildren taught to make the like. She, however, thought he meant to make slaves of them, as Persian ladies were not brought up to work; so that he had to reassure her, and tell her that the distaff, loom, and needle were held to give honor to Greek ladies."—*Miss Yonge.*

Siege of Tyre.—Darius had fled beyond the rivers and

Alexander thought it best to reduce the western part of the empire before following him. The greater part of Syria and Phœnicia submitted to Alexander without opposition. Tyre alone closed her gates against him.

The city was built on an island, half a mile from shore and was fortified by lofty walls, their foundations secured by butresses projecting into the sea. The inhabitants relying upon the security of their situation set him at defiance.

Alexander immediately made preparations to besiege the town, but soon found the task the most difficult one he had undertaken. It was accomplished by the aid of the Sidonian fleet after a siege of seven months. He constructed a causeway two hundred feet wide and half a mile long over which he rolled his ponderous machines and breached the wall, thus carrying the place by desperate assault. "Eight thousand of the inhabitants were slain and thirty thousand sold into slavery, a terrible warning to those cities that should dare to close their gates against the Macedonian."—*Myers*.

Jerusalem.—"From Phœnicia, Alexander marched to Palestine and found no town to resist his progress but Gaza, which was bravely defended by the governor." It was finally taken by storm, and a cruel slaughter was made of the citizens. "Alexander next approached Jerusalem expecting another tedious siege. Instead of this, he beheld a long procession in white bordered with blue coming out of the gates to meet him. All the Priests and Levites, in their robes, came forth, headed by Jaddua, the High Priest, in his beautiful raiment with the golden mitre on his head inscribed with the name

'Holiness unto the Lord.' When Alexander beheld the sight, he threw himself from his horse, and adored the name on the mitre. He told his officers that before he set out from home, when he was considering his journey, just such a form as he now beheld had come and bidden him fear not for he should be led into the East and all Persia should be delivered to him. Then the High Priest took him to the outer court of the temple and showed him the very prophecies of Daniel and Zechariah where his own conquests were foretold."—*Miss Yonge.*

"Judea now belonged to Alexander, but he treated the people well, allowing them to retain their own religion and laws. He excused the payment of tribute once in seven years, that they might obey the law of Moses, in letting the land lie idle every seventh year. They had only exchanged masters, and Alexander treated them, perhaps, more kindly than the Persians had done."—*Edith Ralph.*

"*Egypt* next attracted the attention of Alexander and thither he led his victorious army, but the Egyptians never had been very faithful subjects of the Persians, by whom their country had been oppressed and their religion insulted. They, therefore, submitted to Alexander, and this important country was acquired without the loss of a single man or the shedding of a drop of blood. Ever anxious to forward the interests of commerce, Alexander selected the site of Alexandria as the best place for a commercial city. The wisdom of his choice soon appeared, for the new city in a very few years became one of the most prosperous commercial marts in the world.

"The fame of the temple of Jupiter Ammon, situated in the oasis of the great desert, induced Alexander to pay a visit to this celebrated oracle. He accordingly made his way thither with a chosen band. The Macedonians were astonished at beholding the fertility of the oasis, which seemed like a green island in the sandy ocean."—*Dr. Goldsmith.*

Eighty priests, with maidens dancing about them, came to meet him, bearing the emblem of their god, a golden disc adorned with precious stones and placed in a huge golden ship. Alexander was taken alone to the innermost shrine, where he must have heard much to exalt himself, for ever after this he wore ram's horns on his helmet, which were the sign of the god, and seemed to consider himself no mere man, but the son of Jupiter, like Bacchus or Hercules of old.—*Compiled from Miss Yonge.*

"Alexander then returned across the desert to Memphis, and having provided for the future government of Egypt, brought his army back to Syria."—*Goldsmith.*

Battle of Arbe'la.—The next summer he set out for the East to encounter the Persian army under Darius. "A bridge was thrown across the Euphrates, but the Tigris was forded by the foot soldiers, holding their shields above their heads out of the water."—*Miss Yonge.*

On the other side Darius was waiting with an army over "a million strong, besides being provided with elephants and chariots, armed with scythes. But this army was an inert mass, without spirit or energy, ready to fight, indeed, for their sovereign but as ready to fly when he fell or retreated.

"Alexander came in sight of the enemy at too late an hour, and both armies spent the night on the field of battle. The Macedonians, not being formed in line, were permitted to sleep, but Darius, fearing that if his ranks were disturbed it would be impossible to reorganize such a mighty host, compelled his men to stand to their arms all night."—*Goldsmith.*

"Alexander's general, Parmenio, wished him to take advantage of the darkness and attack the Persians at once; but he only answered, 'it would be base to steal a victory.' When Parmenio came in the morning to say that all was ready, he found his master fast asleep, and asked him how he could rest so calmly with one of the greatest battles in the world before him. 'How could we not be calm,' replied Alexander, 'since the enemy is coming to deliver himself into our hands.'"—*Miss Yonge.*

" Alexander wore in this battle a short coat girt close around him; over that a breast-plate of linen strongly quilted, which he had taken in the battle of Issus. His helmet was of polished iron, and shone like silver. To this was fixed a gorget, set with precious stones. His sword was light and of the finest temper. The belt he wore was superb and was given him by the Rhodians as a mark of respect. In reviewing and exercising he spared Bucephalus, but he rode him in battle, and when he mounted his back it was always a signal for the onset."
—*Goodrich.*

Darius intended to fold the wings of his army around

the Greeks, "but Alexander, foreseeing this, had warned his men to be ready to face about on any side. He then drew them up in shape of a wedge, and broke into the very heart of the Immortal band, and was on the point of taking Darius prisoner when he was called off to assist Parmenio, whose division had been broken, so that the camp was threatened. Alexander's presence soon made the victory complete. Darius, however, had time to escape and was galloping on a swift horse to the Armenian mountains."—*Miss Yonge.*

He was soon afterwards treacherously slain by his own satraps, who were endeavoring to escape from the pursuing Macedonians. "Darius was in the last agony of death when a Macedonian soldier came up and brought him a little water to cool his raging thirst; he expressed great anxiety to see his generous conqueror, and thank him in person for the kindness that had been shown to his mother and family, but before Alexander came up he expired."—*Goldsmith.* "Alexander caused his body to be embalmed and buried in the sepulchers of the Persian kings."—*Miss Yonge.*

Entrance into Babylon.—"Alexander was now declared king of all Asia, and, though this might seem the summit of his glory, it was the point at which his character begins to decline. "He, however, continued his conquests."—*Goodrich.* "He marched in through the brazen gates of Babylon, when the streets were strewn with flowers, and presents of lions and leopards borne forth to greet the conqueror. The great temple of Bel had been partly ruined by the fire-worshiping Persians, and Alexander greatly pleased the Babylonians by decreeing that they might restore it with his aid."—*Miss Yonge.*

Susa and Persepolis.—"After staying thirty days in Babylon, he went on to Susa, where he found the brazen statues which Xerxes had carried away from the sack of Athens. He sent them home again to show the Greeks he had avenged their cause."—*Miss Yonge.* "He also seized incredible quantities of gold and silver ($57,000,-000 it is said), the treasure of the Great King. From Susa his march was to Persepolis, where he secured a treasure twice as great. Here he wreaked vengeance, for all Greece had suffered at the hands of the Persians. Many of the inhabitants were massacred and others sold into slavery; while the palaces of the Persian king were given to the flames. Alexander now assumed the pomp and state of an Oriental monarch, and required the most obsequeous homage from all who approached him."—*Myers.*

The Greeks now wished to return home and keep all of the empire subject to them; but this was not Alexander's plan. His ambition was to spread Greek wisdom and training over all the world, and to rule Persians as well as Greeks for their own good. He permitted the Greeks to return home with pay, rewards, and honors, but he retained his Macedonians. The adoption of the Persian dress and customs, and conferring marks of honor on Persian nobles aroused the jealousy of several of his captains. "There were murmurs and Parmenio was accused of being engaged in a conspiracy and was put to death. It was the first sad stain on Alexander's life, and he fell into a fierce angry mood, being fretted by the murmurs of the Macedonians and harrassed by the difficulties of the wild mountainous countries on the border of Persia where he went to hunt down the last Persians who held out against him."—*Miss Yonge.*

Conquest in Aryan Home.—"After subduing many tribes that dwelt about the Caspian Sea and among the mountainous region of what is now Afghanistan, he boldly conducted his soldiers over the snowy and dangerous passes of the Hindu Kush, and descended into the region described as the first home of the Aryan people."—*Myers.*

"A mountain-fortress on a steep rock surrounded with snow, for a time delayed his progress, its defenders when summoned to yield, tauntlingly asking whether he had winged soldiers." "Irritated by this taunt, Alexander offered large sums to those who would scale the cliff." "Three hundred picked men, driving iron spikes into the ice-bound face of the rock and drawing themselves up with ropes, made the ascent under cover of the night, and at dawn the barbarians surrendered. Among the captives was the Princess Roxana, 'the Pearl of the East,' who became the bride of Alexander."—*Quackenbos.*

Soon after this exploit he was foolish enough to indulge in a wine-drinking banquet, where a quarrel arose between himself and Clitus, his dearest friend, and the favorite companion, who had saved his life at the battle of Gran'icus. Both were flushed with wine, and when Clitus, jealous of the fawning flattery of his Persian subjects, taunted the king of "his inferiority to his father and ascribed the victories to the valor of himself and his brother soldiers, Alexander, stung to madness, seized a javelin and laid the injudicious censurer dead at his feet. Scarcely, however, had he perpetrated the crime when he was seized with remorse; his attendants could with difficulty prevent him from laying violent hands on himself; he was hurried to his chamber, where he remained for three days inconsolable; and it was not without difficulty that his mind was again restored to its wonted composure."—*Goldsmith*.

Alexander in India.—"After having established numerous cities in this remote region and peopled them with captives and followers who had become weary of war, he recrossed the mountains and led his army down upon the rich plains of India."—*Myers.* " Here he received the submission of thirty-five cities, and founded two more, one of which he named Bucephalus, in honor of his noble horse, which died in the midst of battle without a wound."—*Miss Yonge.* " Porus, an Indian monarch of gigantic size and strength, mounted on his elephant, bravely disputed the march of the invaders. Being captured and brought before Alexander he was asked what he desired. 'To be treated as a king,' he replied."—*Quackenbos.* Alexander granted his request, restored his dominions, making him, however, one of his tributaries.

They had now reached the banks of the Hy'phasis, a branch of the Indus, and the conqueror wished to push on to the Ganges, but his Macedonians absolutely refused to go on further, so he was forced to return.

Instead of going directly back he built boats and descended the Indus. At the head of the delta he founded a city called Alexandria, which "was to be to the trade of India what Alexandria on the Nile was to that of Egypt."—*Myers.* Then proceeding to the mouth of the river he and his companions rejoiced to find the sea, though they were amazed at the ebbing and flowing of the tides, never having seen any in their own Mediterranean.

Re-discovery of Sea Route.—"He now dispatched his trusty admiral, Nearchus, with a considerable fleet, to explore the sea, and to determine whether it communicated with the Euphrates. At the same time he resolved to return to Persia along the sea coast, both for the purpose of keeping up a connection with his fleet and subduing the intervening nations. His march thus lay through the ancient Gedrosia, now Beloochistan, a region frightful with burning deserts."—*Myers.* "Their sufferings from thirst, the heat of the sun, and the burning sand exceeded anything they had hitherto experienced, but the sight of their sovereign sharing in their toils, and submitting to equal privations without a murmur, cheered them to fresh exertions."—*Goldsmith.* At length they reached the shores of the Persian Gulf, and to Alexander's unbounded joy, "he was joined by Nearchus, who had made the voyage from the Indus successfully, and thus rediscovered one of the most important maritime routes of the world, the knowledge of which, among the Western nations, was never again to be lost."—*Myers.*

Return March.—The march of the army through Persia was a triumphal procession, and at Susa "he made a nuptial feast for the newly-married people, and nine thousand persons sat down to the entertainment. Each one was honored with a golden cup."—*Goodrich*

Death at Babylon.—"On his return to Babylon Alexander determined to make that place his capital and residence, and set about various plans for carrying this into effect."—*Goodrich.* Before he could accomplish them, and just before setting out upon a new expedition into Arabia, he was seized by a fever, brought on, doubtless, by the unhealthy climate and his own excesses, and died, 323 B. C., in the thirty-second year of his age. "His body was carried to Alexandria, Egypt, and there enclosed in a golden coffin, over which was raised a splendid mausoleum."—*Myers.*

Character of Alexander.—"Thus perished prematurely this extraordinary chieftain in the vigor of manhood and in the midst of ambitious plans. During his short reign of a dozen years he made Macedonia the mistress of half the world. Yet, though lord of this immense empire, he was slave to his own passions. He surrendered himself to dissipation, and in the heat of anger committed deeds that he remembered with remorse.

"Occasionally Alexander displayed unusual greatness of soul, many examples of which have been given. It is told that a cup of water was once offered to him in the desert, but seeing his soldiers gaze upon it with eagerness, he poured it on the ground, lest the sight of his thirst should aggravate the suffering of his men."—*Quackenbos.*

Results of Alexander's Conquests.—"Other invaders have passed over the plains of Asia, both in ancient and modern times, but their career has been like the poison wind of the desert; traceable only by the ruin and desolation that marked their progress. The march of Alexander was not wholly attended by evil, for every invading army must cause calamity, but the monuments of his glorious career were seventy cities founded under his auspices, commercial marts established on all the principal rivers, and improved systems of agriculture and social life taught to wandering tribes."—*Goldsmith.* (See Myers.) As Alexander's son was a helpless infant, the vast dominions were divided among his generals. They soon quarreled, and sanguinary wars desolated the empire.

Greece and Macedonia.—The Greek cities continued to be under the control of the Macedonian kings, but they were never loyal subjects. When the Roman power arose the Macedonians sent aid to Carthage, thus incurring the anger of Rome, which resulted in the subjection to the Italian power (148 B. C.). "The dissensions among the Hellenic people led them to become in the hands of intriguing Rome, weapons first for crushing Macedonia, and then for grinding each other to pieces." *Myers.* Corinth, at this time the most splendid city of all Greece, was taken by the Roman army, and laid in ashes (146 B. C.). Its commercial superiority was transferred to the islands of Rhodes and Delos, and the wonderful works of art, which beautified the city, were carried to Italy.

Thus Ancient Greece expired. Henceforth it was simply a Roman province.

Alexandria, the seaport of Egypt, situated on the Rosetta, mouth of the Nile, was founded by Alexander the

Great just after his conquest of Tyre in (332 B. C.). The wisdom of the choice soon became evident for in a few years Alexandria became the meeting place of the East and the West and one of the most prosperous commercial marts of the world.

When Alexander's empire was divided among his generals Egypt fell to the lot of Ptolemy. He was a wise, clear-headed man, with much of Alexander's spirit of teaching and improving the people under him. The new city of Alexandria was his capital, and here he founded a flourishing Greek kingdom. The Egyptians, protected in their ancient religion, laws, and customs, became faithful subjects. (Having conquered Syria, Phœnicia, and a few other neighboring countries, Ptolemy transported one hundred thousand Jews to Alexandria.) Finding many of their brethren there they readily made themselves at home in Egypt. They had a temple similar to the one at Jerusalem, and for their use the Old Testament was translated into Greek (275–250 B. C.) for even Jews spoke Greek. Thus the Greeks for the first time heard of the true God, and Alexander's dream of blending the races of the East and the West had come to be realized.

Under the rule of the Ptolemies Alexandria became the great emporium of exchange between Asia and Europe. A superb light-house, known as one of the Seven Wonders of the World, stood at the entrance of the harbor to guide the ships of the world, and a canal to the Red Sea facilitated trade with Arabia and India.

That Alexandria might also be an intellectual center, Ptolemy founded the famous museum or college which became the University of the East, and almost as famous as Athens, and established the Alexandrian library. Poets, artists and philosophers were encouraged to settle at Alexandria; and at one time there were as many as fourteen thousand persons in attendance at the University. While wars shook Europe and Asia, scholars of all departments of learning found quiet and safety upon the peaceful banks of the Nile. Greek architects had also contributed to the beauty of the city. Temples, palaces, obelisks and theaters adorned it, and, centrally located in the midst of gardens and fountains, stood the mausoleum erected as Alexander's shrine.

Following the first three Ptolemies were ten weak-minded successors, under whose rule Alexandria commenced to decline. After the death of Cleopatra, the last of the Ptolemies, Egypt became a province of Rome. Alexandria remained a seat of learning during the best days of Rome.

In the seventh century, A. D., it was captured by the Arabs, who brought it under the Mohammedan rule. It is said that "the flames of its four thousand baths were fed for six months with the priceless manuscripts from the library of the Ptolemies." It is now, like all Mohammedan cities, of very little importance in the world, though its harbor is next to Marseilles in size.

PART II.

HISTORY OF ROME.

THE GOLDEN AGE.

Physical Italy.—Italy is a southern peninsula of Europe, lying between the Tuscan and Adriatic seas, and separated from the countries on the north by the Alps, the highest range of mountains in Europe. "These mountains form a semicircle, coming down quite to the sea on the west, thus separating Italy from Gaul, as well as Germany, by a barrier of great difficulty; but on the east they open by low and easy passes to the valleys of the Save and the Danube.

"The great mountain chain of Italy is that of the Apennines, extending southeasterly the whole extent of the peninsula. The mountains of Sicily are a continuation of this chain. This island was, no doubt, a part of the mainland, but was torn from it by some convulsion of nature.

"Italy differs from the other peninsula of Europe, being long and narrow in shape. It stretches into the sea in a general southeasterly direction, at its extremity bending sharply to the south, so as to present, rudely, the shape of a boot, the heel of which is turned toward Greece." The great basin between the Alps and the northern Apennines is drained by the Po, and is one of the most fertile valleys of Europe.

"In Italy proper there are west of the Apennines three principal river systems, the seat in modern times of the three great cities of Florence, Rome, and Naples." The fertile soil of these valleys, combined with the mild climate, influenced by the mountain barriers and the proximity of the ocean, led the early people of Italy to become cultivators of the soil, though the care of cattle was a leading part of their industry. "Barley and spelt were their principal crops; they cultivated the vine at a very early date and received the olive from the Greeks."

"The coast of Italy was not, like Greece, indented with deep bays, hence the people were not originally seamen." The situation of Rome is an admirable one for commerce, and it was from that industry that Rome gained its first impulse to greatness.—*Compiled from Allen.*

Contrast between Greece and Italy. (See page 204; Barnes.)

Founding of Rome.—"There were more than twenty different accounts of the way in which Rome was founded, but they all agree in representing its founder and first king as Romulus, who was believed to be a son of the god Mars."—*Allen; Barnes' Gen. His., page 205.*

"The original city was on the Palatine Hill. This city was called Roma Quadrata, or Square Rome. Some massive walls of this early town have been discovered in recent years. By degrees the town outgrew its walls and spread over the surrounding heights, and then united with a Sabine city on the Quirinal. In the valley between the Palatine and the Quirinal, swampy and subject to overflow, was the Forum or market-place. Beside it, upon a spot somewhat more elevated, a space was enclosed called the Comitium, for assemblies. The citadel of the new city was upon a spur of the Quirinal called the Capitoline."—*Allen*.

Conquest by Etruscans.—The rising city was in its turn conquered by the Etruscans, a people who lived between the Arno and the Tiber, in the country now called Tuscany. These people were great builders, and were skilled in the arts. The rulers which the Etruscans placed upon the throne were called the Tarquins. They added the adjacent heights to the growing capital and enclosed its seven hills within walls that lasted nearly eight centuries. Nearly all the rest of Latium was conquered by them and made tributary to Rome.

The Public Works of the Tarquins.—Rome was for the first time adorned with splendid temples and other public works. The most important were three in number. First, the temple of Jupiter, upon the Capitoline Hill, which was known as the Capitolium.

"As this temple was the central seat of the Roman religion and nationality and was frequently used for meetings of the Senate, the name *capitol* has come to be applied very generally to buildings which are the seat of government. Secondly, a magnificent set of sewers, the principal of which was the one which drained the marshy valley between the hills and rendered the ground fit for the purposes of the Forum and Comitium. In this structure the principle of the arch was employed, which was in use in other parts of Italy also at this early period. These sewers are still in use. Thirdly, the city walls which were now for the first time made to include both the Sabine and the Roman towns."—*Allen*.

Servius Tullius.—These walls were the work of Servius Tullius, the greatest of the Tarquins and one of the most noted of the seven fabled kings of Rome. He was a friend of the common people, or Plebeians, as they were called. "That these might not be oppressed by the senatorial families, or the Patricians, he caused a law to be enacted that the senate could not make a decree without the consent of the Comitia, or the assemby of the people. This was the first step toward that republican liberty which afterwards became the glory of Rome and the world."

Tullius also advocated a plan by which the people should yearly chose their own rulers. "This so angered the house of Tarquin and the Patricians that one of the Tarquins struck Servius dead and was rewarded by being made king. He is known as Tarquinius Superbus, or Tarquin the Proud. He was a hard king, and the people mourned for the good Servius, who had made himself a martyr to their cause, and wished that his days would return."

Some distinguished citizens of Rome sent, as a present to Abraham Lincoln, one of the stones from the wall of Servius. "President Lincoln, it is said, from a modest feeling, hid the stone in a cellar of the White House.

He little dreamed that his own history, which so far had resembled that of Servius Tullius, would also end like that noble Roman's." The stone has since been placed in Lincoln's tomb at Springfield, Illinois.—*Butterworth.*

RISE OF THE REPUBLIC.

Brutus, First Consul.—Tarquin the Proud was so unjust and oppressive that the Romans, headed by a noble Roman named Brutus, rose up and drove Tarquinius and his family without the walls. The republic was then established, 509 B. C., a year after Hippias was driven out of Athens. Two chief magistrates or consuls were chosen every year, and these consuls must be patricians. Brutus, who distinguished himself in expelling the royal family, was chosen one of the first two consuls. The constitution of Servius was adopted, and the senate was restored to its original three hundred, by the addition of members chosen from the richest of the knights (equites), several of whom were plebians.

"The early republic required its consuls or presidents to be men of simple habits and living. When one of the prætors built a costly and pretentious house, the people compelled him to pull it down. They said it indicated an ambition to live in a style above them and would end in royalty.."—*Butterworth.*

During the rule of Brutus, the Tarquins sought to come back again, and many of the Patrician families, not liking the simple freedom of the republic, favored their return. A conspiracy was formed to restore the

Tarquins. "The plot was discovered and the consuls were obliged to condemn the traitors to death." When they were brought before the consuls it was found that the two sons of Brutus were among the number. Would the President condemn his own sons?

When asked what defense they had to make, they only stood and wept in silence.

The senators had compassion on them and cried out: "Let them be banished."

But the father sternly replied, "Executioners, do your office." The officers led out the two sons and scourged and beheaded them before their father's eyes. Thus to disregard his own affections when public interest was concerned was considered a great virtue in the early days of Greece and Rome.

Brutus died fighting the Etruscans, and was mourned a whole year by the matrons of Rome.

Invasion by Lars Porsenna.—Soon after the death of Brutus, a powerful army of Etruscans, under Lars Porsenna, king of Clusium, came to the Tiber to restore the banished Tarquins. "Porsenna defeated the Roman army, and was about to cross the Tiber and occupy the city, when Hora'tius Co'cles took his post on the bridge, and with two brave companions faced the Etruscans. While the three held the opposing host in check, their countrymen hewed down the bridge.—*Quackenbos.*

HORATIUS AT THE BRIDGE.

Lars Porsenna of Clusium—by the Nine Gods he swore
That the great house of Tarquin should suffer wrong no more.
By the Nine Gods he swore it, and named a trysting day,
And bade his messengers ride forth, to summon his array.

East and west and south and north the messengers ride fast,
And tower and town and cottage have heard the trumpet's blast.
Shame on the false Etruscan who lingers in his home
When Porsenna of Clusium is on the march for Rome.

The horsemen and the footmen are pouring in amain,
From many a stately market-place; from many a fruitful plain;
From many a lonely hamlet, which, hid by beech and pine,
Like an eagle's nest, hangs on the crest of purple Apennine.

The harvests of Arretium, this year, old men shall reap;
This year, young boys in Umbro shall plunge the struggling sheep;
And in the vats of Luna, this year, the must shall foam
Round the white feet of laughing girls whose sires have marched to
    Rome.

. . . .

And now hath every city sent up her tale of men;
The foot are fourscore thousand, the horse are thousands ten.
Before the gates of Sutrium is met the great array,
A proud man was Lars Porsenna upon the trysting day.

. . . .

But by the yellow Tiber was tumult and affright;
From all the spacious campaign to Rome men took their flight.
A mile around the city, the throng stopped up the ways,
A fearful sight it was to see, through two long nights and days.

. . . .

Now from the rock Tarpeian could the wan burghers spy
The line of blazing villages red in the midnight sky,
The Fathers of the city, they sat all night and day,
For every hour some horseman came with tidings of dismay.

. . . .

I wis, in all the Senate, there was no heart so bold,
But sore it ached, and fast it beat, when that ill news was told.
Forthwith up rose the Consul, up rose the Fathers all;
In haste they girded up their gowns, and hied them to the wall.

They held a council standing before the River-Gate;
Short time was there, ye may well guess, for musing or debate.
Out spoke the Counsel roundly: "The bridge must straight go down;
For since Janiculum is lost, naught else can save the town."

Just then a scout came flying, all wild with haste and fear:
"To arms! to arms! Sir Consul; Lars Porsenna is here."
On the low hills to westward, the Consul fixed his eye.
And saw the swarthy storm of dust rise fast along the sky.

. . . .

But the Consul's brow was sad and the Consul's speed was low.
And darkly looked he at the wall, and darkly at the foe.
"Their van will be upon us before the bridge goes down;
And if they once may win the bridge, what hope to save the town?"

Then out spake Horatius, the captain of the gate:
"To every man upon this earth death cometh, soon or late.
And how can man die better than facing fearful odds,
For the ashes of his fathers and the temples of his gods?

. . . .

"Hew down the bridge, Sir Consul, with all the speed ye may;
I, with two more to help me, will hold the foe in play.
In yon straight path a thousand may well be stopped by three.
Now, who will stand on either hand, and keep the bridge with me?"

Then out spake Spurius Lartius—a Ramnian proud was he,—
"Lo, I will stand at thy right hand, and keep the bridge with thee."
And out spake strong Herminius—of Titian blood was he,—
"I will abide on thy left side, and keep the bridge with thee."

"Horatius," quoth the Consul, "as thou sayest, so let it be."
And straight against that great array forth went the dauntless three.
For Romans in Rome's quarrel spared neither land nor gold.
Nor son nor wife, nor limb nor life, in the brave days of old.

. . . .

Now while the three were tightening their harness on their backs,
The Consul was the foremost man to take in hand an axe;
And Fathers mixed with Commons seized hatchet, bar, and crow,
And smote upon the planks above, and loosed the props below.

. . . .

The three stood calm and silent, and looked upon the foes,
And a great shout of laughter from all the vanguard rose;
And forth three chiefs came spurring before that deep array;
To earth they sprang, their swords they drew to win the narrow way.

Stout Lartius hurled down Annus into the stream beneath;
Herminius struck at Seius, and clove him to the teeth;
At Picus brave Horatius darted one fiery thrust;
And the proud Umbrian's gilded arms clashed in the bloody dust.

. . . .

But all Etruria's noblest felt their hearts sink to see
On the earth the bloody corpses, in the path the dauntless three.
And from the ghastly entrance, where those bold Romans stood,
The bravest shrank like boys who rouse an old bear in the wood.

. . . .

But meanwhile axe and lever have manfully been plied,
And now the bridge hangs tottering above the boiling tide.
"Come back, come back, Horatius!" loud cried the Fathers all;
"Back, Lartius! back, Herminius! back, ere the ruin fall!"

Back darted Spurius Lartius; Herminius darted back;
And, as they passed, beneath their feet they felt the timbers crack;
But when they turned their faces, and on the farther shore
Saw brave Horatius stand alone, they would have crossed once more.

But, with a crash like thunder, fell every loosened beam,
And, like a dam, the mighty wreck lay right athwart the stream;
And a long shout of triumph rose from the walls of Rome,
As to the highest turret tops splashed the yellow foam.

And, like a horse unbroken when first he feels the rein,
The furious river struggled hard, and tossed his tawny mane,
And burst the curb, and bounded, rejoicing to be free,
And battlement, and plank, and pier, whirled headlong to the sea.

Alone stood brave Horatius, but constant still in mind;
Thrice thirty thousand foes before, and the broad flood behind.
"Down with him!" cried false Sextus, with a smile on his pale face,
"Now yield thee," cried Lars Posenna, "now yield thee to our grace."

Round turned he, as not deigning those craven ranks to see;
Naught spake he to Lars Porsena, to Sextus naught spake he;
But he saw on Palatinus the white porch of his home,
And he spake to the noble river that rolls by the towers of Rome.

"O Tiber! Father Tiber! to whom the Romans pray,
A Roman's life, a Roman's arms, take thou in charge this day!"
So he spake, and, speaking, sheathed the good sword by his side,
And, with his harness on his back, plunged headlong in the tide.

No sound of joy or sorrow was heard from either bank;
But friends and foes, in dumb surprise, stood gazing where he sank;
And when above the surges they saw his crest appear,
Rome shouted, and e'en Tuscany could scarce forbear to cheer.

But fiercely ran the current, swollen high by months of rain;
And fast his blood was flowing; and he was sore in pain,
And heavy with his armor, and spent with changing blows,
And oft they thought him sinking—but still again he rose.

Never, I ween, did swimmer, in such an evil case,
Struggle through such a raging flood safe to the landing place;
But his limbs were borne up bravely by the brave heart within,
And our good Father Tiber bare bravely up his chin.

"Curse on him?" quoth false Sextus; "will not the villain drown?
But for his stay, ere close of day we should have sacked the town!"
"Heaven help him!" quote Lars Porsenna, " and bring him safe to shore;
For such a gallant feat of arms was never seen before."

And now he feels the bottom—now on dry earth he stands;
Now round him throng the Fathers to press his gory hands.
And, now with shouts and clapping, and noise of weeping loud,
He enters through the River-Gate, borne by the joyous crowd.

They gave him of the corn-land that was of public right
As much as two strong oxen could plough from morn till night;
And they made a molten image, and set it up on high,
And there it stands unto this day to witness if I lie.

It stands in the Comitium, plain for all folk to see;
Horatius in his harness, halting upon one knee;
And underneath is written, in letters all of gold,
How valiantly he kept the bridge in the brave days of old.

—Macaulay.

Lars Porsenna continued the siege until the Romans suffered from hunger, nevertheless they refused to yield. A youth by the name of Caius Marius asked permission to go to the enemy's camp. There he sought to kill Lars Porsenna, but mistaking one of the counselors for the king, struck him dead. He was seized and brought before Lars Porsenna. When asked why he committed the deed he replied, that Rome might be free. "Torture him," was the command. Without hesitation he walked up to the fire and unflinchingly held his bare hand in the flames until the flesh was consumed. To the astonished Etruscans he said that Rome was full of men as brave as himself. He was allowed to return to Rome, and Lars Porsenna soon after made a treaty of peace with the Romans and Tarquin died in exile.

Early Days of the Republic.—We now pass from the Golden Age of tradition and fable to the real life of the Roman Republic. In the early days the two consuls or presidents, who were elected yearly, had the supreme power. The senate at first could give counsel only; it was not till a later time that it became a law-making body. The consuls wore all the insignia of royalty which they had adopted from the Etruscans, with the exception of the crown. They performed the duties of their office while seated on a throne, dressed in purple robes and bearing ivory scepters surmounted by golden eagles. They made the laws, led the people in war, and judged them in peace. When acting as judges they were attended by twelve lictors, who bore on their shoulders as a symbol of authority an ax tied in a bundle of rods. The consuls were elected by the patricians, and were not allowed to serve a second term without waiting a number of years. It was the custom for a person who was seeking a high public office to dress in white, hence our word candidate, from the Latin *Candidus* (white).

The Struggle between the Plebeians and the Patricians.—The plebeians or common people were those who were not descendants of the first settlers of Rome. They tilled the lands and paid enormous taxes to the patricians, served in the army without pay, yet were forbidden the rights of citizens, and not allowed to intermarry with the patricians. While absent in the wars, their farms remained untilled, or were plundered by the enemy. When they returned, they were forced to borrow money to buy seed, tools, and food, thus becoming debtors to the patricians. If they did not meet their payments, they could be sold as slaves, or thrown into the debtor's prison.

An aged prisoner once escaped from prison and appeared before the people. His venerable aspect and pitiable condition demanded the attention of all. His clothes were ragged and his face pallid from long confinement and meager diet. Nevertheless the people knew him as one who had won military distinction, and who had once held the rank of centurion. They were touched with pity and recounted his brave deeds, wondering at his forlorn condition. He bared his breast and showed the scars of many a battle-field. When a crowd had gathered round, and demanded why he appeared thus, he told his pitiful story. He had served in the Sabine wars. His farm was plundered by the enemy, his cattle driven off, his house burned and his crops destroyed, everything of value was gone. The taxes became due, debts were contracted which were multiplied by the exorbitant interest. He fell a victim to the inhumanity of his creditors. He was cast into prison, not an ordinary prison, but a dungeon, only relieved by the hard labor of the work-house. In proof of his statements he exhibited the marks of recent scourging on his back.

The people listened with horror, becoming so enraged, that at last they marched off in a body to the Sacred Mount, and threatened to build a new city for themselves.

At this time news came that a tribe of people called Volscians were on their way to attack Rome. The patricians were now alarmed, and not without cause, for the plebeians were ready to join the enemy. The senate sent summons; the people knew their power and refused to fight.

Menenius Agrippa.—There was at this time in Rome a very wise man named Agrippa, who was loved and respected by all. When asked his opinion concerning the struggle between the patricians and plebeians, he recited to them this fable:

"Once upon a time the different organs of the body had a discussion as to their work. The head, heart, hands, and feet, all thought that they were working to support the stomach in idleness. The head complained that it had to think to feed it; the hands, that they had to labor for it; the feet, that they must carry it. They agreed to cease their labors and no more associate with an organ so lowly. The hands refused to labor; the feet would not move; the teeth would not chew the food; but they soon found out their mistake. Their strength went from them; they became poor and helpless. Thus they found how much they were dependent upon the stomach.

"So," said the wise man, "society is made up of different ranks, each necessary to the welfare of the others; all must have the respect and honor due to them."

Tribunes of the People.—Both parties were touched by the story and were willing to make concessions. It was agreed that there should be two tribunes of the people who should be present outside of the assembly to guard the rights of the common people. If any unjust law should be passed, the tribunes could shout their veto through the open door. Their persons were to be sacred and their houses were to stand open day and night, as places of refuge for all the oppressed.

The Decemvirs.—The tribunes being ignorant of the laws, were often unable to fulfill the duties of their office. They, therefore, demanded that the laws be made public. Ten men, called decemvirs, were appointed, whose duty it should be to revise and publish a code of laws, also to govern in place of the consuls and tribunes.

The Laws of the Twelve Tables.—The decemvirs compiled twelve tables of laws, which formed the basis of all legislation for many centuries. They were written on tablets of brass and hung up in the forum, where all could read them. Every school-boy, as late as Cicero's time, learned them by heart.

Appius Claudius.—The Historian Livy tells how the decemvirs fell into dishonor. At first they governed well, but when they were chosen for the second term, Appius Claudius was the only one re-elected. All was now changed; tyranny reigned. Two new tables of oppressive laws were added to the former tables. At the end of the year, no new election was called, for the decemvirs ruled in defiance of the senate and people. Many leading citizens feared for their lives and fled from the city.

One day as Appius Claudius passed through the forum he saw the beautiful daughter of Virginius, a plebeian and officer of the army. Upon inquiring, he learned that her name was Virginia, and that she was engaged to marry a young plebeian. Charmed with her beauty, he resolved to make her his own. He directed his client to abduct her, claiming that she was a child of one of his slaves and not the true daughter of Virginius.

The case came before the decemvirs for trial, Claudius, of course, deciding in favor of his client. Upon hearing the fate of his child, Virginius drew her to one side, as if to bid her farewell. Suddenly seizing a butcher's knife from a booth near by, he stabbed her to the heart, crying, "Thus only can I make thee free."

Appius ordered Virginius to be seized; but he was protected by his friends, who escorted him to the city gates. He escaped to the camp, and aroused the soldiers to vengeance.

Once again the plebeians rose against the patricians and the decemvirs were forced to resign. The former government of consuls and tribunes was renewed. Appius, in despair, killed himself.

Triumph of the Plebs.—The strife between the patricians and plebeians continued through many centuries, marked by only a few bloody contests, but by continual gain on the part of the people. Step by step they pushed their demands for equal privileges with the patricians, until in 300 B. C., nearly two centuries after the republic was established, Rome possessed a democratic government, the highest offices being open to the plebeians. Civil concord brought with it a period of civic virtue and heroic greatness, when "To be a Roman was greater than to be a king."

Foreign Wars.—We have already referred to the foreign wars which disturbed Rome during the struggle for political freedom. Many beautiful legends are connected with these wars, which possess all the dignity if not all the truth of history.

Coriolanus.—In the war with the Volscians, a patrician youth named Caius Marcius gained great renown. When the Romans were besieging the city of Carioli, the Volscians made a sally, but were driven back by Marcius, who pursued them within the walls. He hewed his way out of the gates and admitted the Romans, thus winning the city.

All bleeding from his wounds, he was brought before the consul, who placed a crown upon his head, and said: "Henceforth thou shalt be called Coriolanus." The consul then offered him his share of the spoils in slaves. He chose but one, and then, to the astonishment of all, gave him his liberty.

But Coriolanus was not popular, for he was no friend to the plebeians. Soon after, in a time of famine, when grain was brought from Sicily, he refused to sell any to the plebeians unless they would submit to the patricians. The tribunes, indignant, sought to bring him to trial, but he fled from the city, leaving his mother, wife, and children, and took refuge with the despised Volscians.

Rousing the Volscians, he returned at the head of an army and besieged Rome. The city was in great peril. As a last resort the mothers of Rome resolved to appeal to him. Dressed in the deepest mourning, they passed out of the city gates, headed by the mother and wife of Coriolanus and his own little ones. When they reached the camp, his mother prostrated herself at his feet, saying, "If you come to destroy Rome, begin with me." The appeal touched his heart, and he exclaimed, "Mother, thou hast saved Rome, but lost thy son."

His words were fulfilled. Having ordered a retreat, he is said to have been slain by the angry Volscians.

Cincinnatus.—Another noted patrician living at this time was Cincinnatus, so named because of his curly hair. He lived in a simple way on his farm of four acres, but was known and respected even by the plebeians as a man of sound and just judgment.

One day news came that the consul and his army were surrounded in a deep valley by the Æquians, a neighboring tribe. The people met in council. Who should deliver them in this hour of great peril? Who had sufficient wisdom and prudence? Alas! there seemed to be no one. At last some one proposed the name of Cincinnatus for dictator. It was received with great approval, and messengers immediately summoned him. They found him plowing, assisted by his wife.

We are told that he washed his face, donned his toga, and started in a boat towards Rome.

There he took the lead of a volunteer army, bidding every man carry twelve wooden stakes. That very night he surrounded the enemy's camp with a palisade. Minucius, the consul, hearing the Roman war-cry, renewed the attack with vigor. When morning dawned, the Æquians perceived they had been surrounded and all was lost. "They were forced to surrender and pass under the yoke."

Cincinnatus had saved his country; all honors awaited him. He was awarded a golden crown. Refusing all, he resigned his dictatorship and went back to his little farm on the Tiber.

Marcus Camillus.—"We now come to the most interesting story of the palmy days of the republic." Encouraged by the successes in subduing the neighboring tribes, the Romans determined to rid themselves of their most formidable rival, the Etruscan city of Veii. The siege lasted, with varying fortunes, for ten years, when it was at last concluded by dictator Marcus Camillus, by mining under its walls. The most cruel revenge was then taken upon the inhabitants. The men were put to death; the women and children sold into slavery; nothing was left but the bare walls and deserted buildings of the once flourishing city.

Wishing to punish the city of Falerii, which had aided the Veientes, Camillus appeared before that city. Now it happened that there was an ambitious schoolmaster who had in his charge the sons of the chief families of Falerii. One day, pretending to give them exercise, he took the boys without the gates and conducted them to the Roman camp. Camillus was so enraged at this treachery that he scorned to take advantage of it. Tying the hands of the schoolmaster behind his back, he gave the boys whips and bade them flog their master back to the city. The Falerians, moved by such a display of honor on the part of the Romans, surrendered. The triumph of Camillus was complete, and he entered Rome in all the splendor of a god. His face was covered with vermilion and he was borne in a chariot drawn by four white horses.

Forgetful of the offering to the gods, which must always be a tenth part of the booty, he incurred the distrust of the people. He was accused of pride and appropriating to himself the bronze gates of the city of Veii. The tribunes impeached him and he departed from the city into voluntary exile, praying that Rome might yet need his help.

The Gallic Invasion.—The time soon came. "Five years later a great alarm came to Rome. There was a barbarian nation in the north called the Gauls. They had blue eyes, yellow hair, and strong arms; they went naked down to the waist, and their bands or armies were fearful to look upon. They had driven the Etruscans away from the fertile lands of the Po, and had crossed the Apennine Mountains and were facing Rome. They came like a hurricane, and nothing could withstand them. The Roman senators, true to their city, resolved to die in their seats."—*Butterworth.* They dressed themselves in their robes of state and sat down like so many statues in their ivory chairs of magistracy to await death. The barbarians, hurrying through the deserted streets, at length came to the forum. For a moment they stood amazed at the sight of those solemn faces, so like unto gods in the magnificence of their attire and the majesty of their looks. One of the Gauls put out his hand reverently to stroke the white beard of an aged senator, when the indignant Roman smote him with his ivory staff. The spell was broken and the senators were ruthlessly massacred. The city was then pillaged and burned.

A Roman force still held the capitol, which was besieged by the Gauls for some months. One night a party of Gauls stealthily clambered up the steep ascent of the Capitoline Hill, one of them reaching the highest ledge, when the cackling of the sacred geese in the temple of Juno gave the alarm. Marcus Manlius, a brave patrician, was aroused by the noise, and rushed out just in time to dash the foremost Gaul over the precipice. Other Romans rallied to the aid of Manlius, and the invaders were repulsed. Thus it came to be a proverb that "Rome was saved by the cackling of a goose!"

This attempt having failed the Gauls began to weary of the siege and agreed to accept a ransom of a thousand pounds of gold. The money was collected with great difficulty by taking the treasures of the temples and the jewels contributed by the Roman women. When the Romans complained of the scales being false, Brennus, the Gallic chief, flung his sword among the weights, insolently exclaiming, "Woe to the vanquished!"

Meanwhile a messenger had been to Camillus, the

exiled dictator, offering him the dictatorship and beseeching him to come to the rescue of the city. Hastily gathering together an army, he is said to have arrived just in season to seize the treasures about to be delivered to the Gauls, and bid défiance to Brennus and his host, saying, "Rome is to be bought with iron, not gold."

The Gauls, dismayed by so formidable an enemy, retired from the city. Camillus pursued them, and not a man escaped to tell how low the city had fallen on that eventful day.

Rome Rebuilt.—Camillus was named the second founder of Rome. He it was who persuaded them to rebuild their city on the hills made glorious by their ancestors, rather than to forsake their sacred altars to occupy the well-built city of Veii. "As soon as it was decided that they should remain in their old home, they energetically went to work with bricks, which were provided by the city without cost, and the stone obtained from the dismantled city of Veii. So little care was observed in regard to the course of streets and sewers, that Rome was a network of very narrow, crooked streets, with high houses, and remained so until after the great fire in the time of Nero.—*Allen.*

Camillus's Speech to the Romans.—(By Livy.)—"My countrymen, we hold a city founded under auspices and with solemn inauguration; there is no spot within its walls that is not full of a divine presence and hallowed associations. The days on which our great sacrifices recur are not more strictly fixed than the places where they are to be offered. Will you desert all these objects of adoration, public and private, my fellow-citizens?

"Some will say, perhaps, that we can fulfill these sacred duties at Veii, or send our own priests from thence to perform them here. Neither can be done without breaking our religious obligations. What shall I say of the eternal Fire of Vesta, and of that image of Pallas, which Æneas brought from Troy, preserved in the guardianship of her temple as the pledge of our empire? What of your sacred shields, O great Mars and Father Quirinus? Is it your will to forsake and leave to desecration all those hallowed symbols, old as the city herself, some even older than her foundation?

. . . .

"If in this whole city no better or more commodious dwelling could be erected than that hut in which our founder lived,—were it not better to live in huts like shepherds and peasants, amidst your own shrines and household gods, than go into this national exile? . . . Does our affection or our native place depend on walls and beams? For mine own part, when I was late in exile, I confess that as often as my native city came into my thoughts, there rose before my eyes all this,—these hills, these plains, yon Tiber, and the scene so familiar to my sight, and the bright sky under which I was born and brought up. O Roman countrymen! rather let these things move you now by the love you bear them, to stay where you are, than wring your hearts with regret for them hereafter! Not without cause did gods and men fix on this spot to found a city : health-giving hills, a river nigh at hand, to bring in food from all inland places, to receive supplies by sea; the sea itself handy for commerce, yet not so near as to expose the city to hostile fleets; a spot central to all Italy, adapted beyond all others for the growth of a great state."

"Camillus was six times made dictator, and proved himself superior to all of his enemies, and died in honored old age."—*Butterworth*.

Several important military reforms are believed to have been the work of Marcus Camillus, the great commander of his age. Heretofore, the Roman army had been a militia, serving without pay; now it became a body of paid troops.

"The early Roman army, like that of the Greeks, was a phalanx, that is, a compact body forming a continuous line without breaks or intervals. An army drawn up in this order and armed with long spears, was almost invincible in defense; but it could not move with ease or precision, except upon level ground, and was unsuited to attack." The legion, which is thought to have been introduced by Camillus, was the opposite of the phalanx, being flexible instead of compact. The army was formed into three ranks, the companies of one standing behind the spaces of that in front; by this it was possible to withdraw the front line and advance those in the rear through the spaces between those in front.—*Allen*.

Rome was now mistress of Central Italy, and was considered the common defender of the neighboring nations.

War with Pyrrhus.—A few years later nearly all the Greek cities of Southern Italy had acknowledged the growing power of the imperial city. Tarentum, however, a commercial city of great wealth and enterprise, now made a last effort to check the dominion of Rome.

The Tarentines, wishing to keep the field of traffic to themselves, required the Romans to keep their ships of war away from the southern coast. In direct violation of a treaty to that effect, a Roman fleet appeared off the harbor of Tarentum. War followed and the Tarentines, too lazy to defend themselves, applied to Pyrrhus, king of Epirus, one of the ablest and most ambitious princes since the time of Alexander. Pyrrhus, overjoyed at the prospect of conquering the Western world, sailed with a large army and, what proved of more importance than any other part of the army, a troop of twenty elephants. The compact phalanx of the Greeks was at first more than a match for the Roman legion and the unwonted sight of the elephants threw the Roman cavalry into confusion. Thus Pyrrhus won two hard fought battles, but he is reported to have said, "Another such a victory would compel me to return to Epirus alone." As he surveyed the field of carnage after his first triumph and beheld the stalwart forms of the dead Romans with their resolute features and not a single wound behind he exclaimed, "Had I such soldiers, how easily could I become master of the world." He realized the impossibility of conquering such a nation of heroes and accordingly sent his friend Cineas, an ambassador, who was famous for his powers of persuasion, to arrange terms of peace. So successful was he with his honeyed speech, the senate were about to yield when the aged and blind Appius Claudius caused himself to be led into the assembly and declared that Rome should never treat for peace so long as a foreign enemy stood upon the soil of Italy. The presents sent to the senators and their families after the Greek custom of commencing negotiations were haughtily refuséd by the Roman wives. Cineas on returning told Pyrrhus that Rome was like a great temple, and the Roman senate an assembly of kings. Soon after this event an embassy of the Romans headed by Caius Fabricius Luscinus was sent to Pyrrhus to treat concerning the exchange of prisoners. Fabricius had long been a pattern to his countrymen for his contentment amid poverty. To try his integrity Pyrrhus offered him presents; but they were refused. Then the king resolved to break his lofty spirit. " He summoned Fabricius to a conference in the royal tent which was divided into two parts by a curtain.

"As they were conversing, the curtain suddenly dropped, and an enormous elephant that had been hidden behind it raised his trunk over the Roman's head and trumpeted.

"But Fabricius was not to be thus frightened. He turned to the king and said: 'I am not to be bribed by your gold nor frightened by your beast.' "—*Butterworth*.

Pyrrhus was gratified to find so much integrity and courage in a barbarian, as he called the Roman, and, as a mark of his regard, he released all the Roman prisoners without ransom.

Fabricius was chosen consul the next year. In the next campaign, while the two armies were approaching each other, a letter was brought to Fabricius from the physician of Pyrrhus, offering to poison the king for a proper reward. The honest old Roman was indignant at such a wicked proposal, and sent off the messengers at once to inform Pyrrhus of the plot against his life. Pyrrhus, filled with admiration at the nobility and generosity of Fabricius and his friends, gave up all thought of continuing the struggle and retired into Sicily to defend the Greek city of Syracuse against the Carthaginians. At first he was everywhere successful; but finally fortune turned against him, and in desperation he returned to Italy to engage in a final struggle with the Romans. When marching at night to attack the Romans, his army lost their way in a dense forest, and it was broad day when they came in sight of the Roman force. Wearied as they were, they were obliged to join battle at once, thus giving the Romans the advantage. The elephants, their last hope, were sent into the thick of the combat, but this time the Romans were prepared for them and showered them with arrows headed with blazing tow. The huge animals, maddened with pain and terror, turned and trampled on their masters, who, panic-stricken, took to flight. The rout was complete, and soon afterwards Pyrrhus, collecting his shattered forces, returned to Epirus, leaving only a small garrison at Tarentum. "He had scarcely embarked before Tarentum surrendered to the Romans (272 B. C.). This ended the struggle for the mastery of Italy. Rome was now mistress of all the peninsula south of the Arnus and the Rubicon." It was now her care to make a strong union of her possessions by a perfect network of colonies and military roads.

The Roman Government.—The city of Rome was the center of all executive authority and alone possessed the power to declare war, make peace, and coin money. The cities of the conquered territory, as a rule, retained their right of local self-government, but must furnish their quota of troops for the Roman army. Beyond this requirement no tribute or tax was demanded.

There were three classes of people in this vast commonwealth : first, Roman citizens ; second, Latins ; third, Italians or allies. The Roman citizens included, at first, the free inhabitants of the territory of Rome proper and were divided into thirty-three tribes. To them alone belonged the right of meeting in the forum to enact laws and vote for consuls, etc. Included in this class were the Roman colonists, who were sent to found new Romes in every conquered state, and whose sole military duty it was to protect the sea-coast. The Latins, or second class, embracing the people of many of the conquered towns, were allowed to govern themselves in local concerns, but not to take part in the public affairs of Rome. The Italians, or allies, were the people of those cities who had bound themselves by treaty to contribute regular contingents to the Roman army, but were otherwise independent.

The period which we have now reached is the grandest one in Roman history. Roman peasants still lived on their little farms of three or four acres, just as their ancestors had done, and their frugal industry had converted many a barren field into a fruitful garden. Roman citizenship, at this time, had a might and a meaning, which, as the Roman power extended, was eagerly sought for by every person and city. It was constantly held out as a reward for faithful service to the republic. (Acts XXII, 25; XXIII, 27; XXV, 11–21.

Only those Roman citizens of the city of Rome itself and the vicinity were enabled to exercise the right of suffrage in the Roman assemblies. The modern system of representation, by which other cities could take part in the government of the republic, was never conceived of by the Romans. They knew no form of government except the free city and the despotic empire of the Orient; and when the city government fell they could do nothing but establish the empire.

Military Roads.—During this period, that system of military roads was commenced which united all parts of Italy and, eventually, the most distant provinces by an easy and familiar intercourse. The primary object of these roads, however, was to facilitate the marches of the legions. "They ran in a direct line from one city to another, with very little respect for the obstacles either of nature or private property. Mountains were perforated and bold arches thrown over the most rapid of the streams. The middle part of the road was raised into a terrace, which commanded the adjacent country, consisted of several strata of sand, gravel, and cement, and was paved with large stones, or, in some places near the capital, with granite. Such was the solid construction of the Roman highways, whose firmness has not entirely yielded to the effort of fifteen centuries.

"The advantage of receiving the earliest intelligence and of conveying their orders with celerity, induced the emperors of a later time to establish posts on all the roads. Houses were everywhere erected at a distance only of five or six miles ; each of them was constantly provided with forty horses, and by the help of these relays, it was easy to travel a hundred miles in a day along the Roman roads."—*Gibbon.*

The most celebrated of these ancient roads is the *Appian Way*, which extends from the Roman forum into Southern Italy, a distance of three hundred and fifty miles. Its foundations were laid 312 B. C. by Appius Claudius, the blind.

THE PUNIC WARS.

We now come to the struggle between Rome and Carthage, called the " Punic Wars " from *Pœni*, meaning Phœnicians. In this struggle of more than one hundred years the Aryan and Semitic races contended for the mastery of the world. When Rome completed her conquest of Southern Italy she stood face to face with Carthage. Pyrrhus is said to have exclaimed as he left Sicily : "What a beautiful field we leave for the Romans and Carthaginians."

Carthage, the rival city of Rome, was situated ten miles from the present city of Tunis. It was one of those colonies established by the Phœnicians long before Rome was founded. When Phœnicia lost its importance Carthage became a second Tyre. Utica, Cadiz, and other Phœnician cities of Africa and Spain acknowledged her leadership, and at the time Rome became "Mistress of Italy" the colonies and fortresses of Carthage were scattered over the islands and shores of the Western Mediterranean. Her war galleys swept over the seas, and so complete was the dominion of the proud city that she boasted "that the Romans should not be permitted even to wash their hands in the Mediterranean."

Comparison of Rome and Carthage (See Allen and Myers)—**Origin of the First Punic War.**—The islands of Sardinia, Corsica, and the Balearic Isles were under the power of Carthage, and for centuries the Carthaginians and Greeks had contended for the possession of Sicily. The Romans had never set foot on the island. A slight pretext now served to involve them in the struggle. A horde of Italian pirates had seized Messana. "The king of Syracuse threatened to expel them, and they appealed to Rome for help. The Romans hesitated, but when they saw that the Carthaginian power in Sicily was a menace to their own coast they resolved to possess Sicily as a protection against invasion."—*Butterworth.*

The Greeks and Carthaginians at first united to expel the insolent newcomers, but the Romans were everywhere successful, and obtained a sure foothold on the island. The king of Syracuse finding that he was on the losing side hastened to make friends with the Romans, and continued their ally for a quarter of a century. Soon after this the Romans became masters of the entire island except a few maritime ports which they could not conquer as long as the Carthaginian navy had command of the sea.

Rome's First Fleet.—The Roman senate, not content with a partial success, was determined to rule the sea as well as the land. Rome must have a fleet. A stranded Phœnician vessel was taken as a model, and in sixty days' time one hundred and thirty vessels were built by the

Romans. The ships were provided with draw-bridges, so that their disciplined soldiers could rush upon the enemy's deck and come at once to a hand-to-hand contest. In four years' time the Romans had established their supremacy on the sea by two great naval victories over the Carthaginians.

Romans Cross the Sea.—A few years later the senate sent an army into Africa led by the consul Regulus. For a time he carried all before him and Carthage seemed about to fall when a Spartan took command and overthrew the Roman army with great slaughter, taking Regulus prisoner.

The Romans were forced to evacuate Africa, and, for several years, the war dragged on, with a few successes on the island of Sicily, but disaster after disaster on the sea. Four Roman fleets had been destroyed, three of them being shattered by storms. At last Hamilcar took command of the Carthaginian forces on the island of Sicily and conducted the war with such skill that Rome trembled for the safety of her Italian possessions. A fleet of two hundred vessels was hastily built and equipped by private subscription. A naval battle was fought which resulted in the overwhelming defeat of the Carthaginians. They now sued for peace, the conditions of which were the cession of Sicily to Rome and the payment of 3,200 talents (about $4,000,000) as war indemnity. Thus ended the First Punic War (241 B. C.), after a period of twenty-four years.

The temple of Janus was now closed for the first time since the days of Numa.

Story of Regulus.—In this war a remarkable example of Roman honor was added to the grand tales of old. Like Cincinnatus, Regulus was a plain man with great good sense and strength of character. He also tilled his simple farm and did not seek for a high office. He was respected by all classes of people, and at the time of the first Punic war was made consul. His office compelled him to assume command of the army. He enlarged the Roman fleet to more than three hundred war vessels, defeated the Carthaginians and landed his army on the Carthaginian shore.

As he was about to advance on Carthage a messenger from Rome came to him and said :

"Your family are suffering and need you ; a slave has run away with the farm tools, and your wife and children know not what to do."

Regulus asked to be relieved of his command that he might return to their assistance, but the senate ordered him to proceed, promising to care for his family. Regulus met with continued success, and would have conquered Carthage had not the Carthaginians been reinforced by a large body of Greek soldiers. This time the Greek general placed one hundred elephants in the van, and again the Roman army was thrown into a panic, as the elephants rushed upon them. A complete defeat followed, and Regulus himself was taken prisoner.

After being kept in confinement a long time, he was selected to carry proposals of peace to the Romans. They asked him :

"Will you swear to return if the senate refuse to make peace ?"

"I will pledge you my honor to return," said Regulus.

When Regulus reached Rome he refused to enter the gates of the city. "I am no longer a Roman citizen," he said, "but a Carthaginian slave. I am an old man, and am not worth exchanging as a prisoner."

He stated the terms of the proposed peace, but, to the amazement of all, he urged that they be rejected as unworthy of the glory and honor of Rome. Then, without visiting his home, he turned his back on the walls of Rome forever, and passed away from the shadows of the Seven Hills, admired by all who held honor more sacred than life. A cruel death awaited him at the hands of the enraged Carthaginians. So perished this martyr to his word and his country, but his name is enrolled with Rome's undying heroes.

REGULUS BEFORE THE SENATE.

Urge me no more; your prayers are vain
   And even the tears ye shed;
When I can lead to Rome again
   The bands that once I led;
When I can raise your legions slain
On swarthy Libya's fatal plain,
   To vengeance from the dead;
Then will I seek once more a home,
And lift a freeman's voice in Rome!

Accursed moment! when I awoke
   From faintness all but death,
And felt the coward conqueror's yoke
   Like venomed serpents wreath
Round every limb; if lip and eye
Betrayed no sign of agony,
   Inly I cursed my breath;
Wherefore, of all that fought, was I
The only wretch that could not die?

To darkness and to chains consigned,
　　The captive's fighting doom
I recked not; could they chain the mind,
　　Or plunge the soul in gloom?
And there they left me, dark and lone,
Till darkness had familiar grown;
　　Then from that living tomb
They led me forth, I thought, to die;
Oh! in that thought was ecstasy!

But no! kind Heaven had yet in store
　　For me, a conquered slave,
A joy I thought to feel no more,
　　Or feel but in the grave.
They deemed, perchance, my haughtier mood
Was quelled by chains and solitude;
　　That he who once was brave—
Was I not brave?—had now become
Estranged from honor as from Rome.

They bade me to my country bear
　　The offers these have borne;
They would have trained my lips to swear,
　　Which never yet have sworn.
Silent their base commands I heard,
At length I pledged a Roman's word,
　　Unshrinking to return.
I go, prepared to meet the worst,
But I shall gall proud Carthage first.

They sue for peace; I bid you spurn
　　The gilded bait they bear;
I bid you still, with aspect stern,
　　War—ceaseless war—declare.
Fools as they were, could not mine eyes,
Through their dissembled calmness, spy
　　The struggles of despair?
Else had they sent this wasted frame
To bribe you to your country's shame?

Your land—(I must not call it mine;
  No country has the slave;
His father's name he must resign,
  And even his father's grave—
But this not now)—beneath her lies
Proud Carthage and her destinies;
  Her empire o'er the wave
Is yours; she knows it well, and you
Shall know, and make her feel it, too.

Ah, bend your brows, ye ministers
  Of coward hearts, on me;
Ye know no longer it is hers,
  The empire of the sea;
  Ye know her fleets are far and few;
Her bands a mercenary crew;
  And Rome, the bold and free,
Shall trample on her prostrate towers,
Despite your weak and wasted powers.

One path alone remains for me;
  My vows were heard on high;
Thy triumphs, Rome, I shall not see,
  For I return to die.
Then tell me not of hope or life;
I have in Rome no chaste, fond wife,
  No smiling progeny;
One word concentres for the slave—
Wife, children, country, ALL—the Grave.
          —*Rev. Thomas Dale.*

Rome's First Provinces.—Sicily now became Rome's first province. The seizure of Sardinia and Corsica was soon after accomplished, and that system of provincial government established which in time made every district in Europe, Asia, and Africa, lying within reach of the Roman legions, become tributary to Rome. According to this provincial system the people outside of Italy were held strictly as subjects. Their lands were not considered their own, but as belonging to Rome. A Roman governor, with absolute power, was appointed to rule over each province, and a heavy tribute was exacted. It can be easily understood that as the Roman character fell from its ideal of honor, that the province soon became an object of plunder and profit to the governor and his friends.

During the peace of twenty-three years between the First and Second Punic Wars, Rome was engaged in subduing the pirates of the Adriatic and the Gauls, who had again begun their ravages. This time the well-trained legions defeated the Gauls with great slaughter, and all northern Italy to the foot of the Alps submitted to the Roman authority. At this time Greece entered into an alliance with the Romans and extended an invitation for them to participate in the Isthmian games. The Athenians hailed the people of the West as kinsmen and heroes, and gave them the freedom of the city. This was the beginning of the intercourse of Rome with the nations of the East.

Second Punic War.—While the Romans were thus extending their sway in Italy and its neighborhood, the Carthaginians were equally active in strengthening their power in the West. Hamilcar was sent into Spain to conquer the peninsula. For nine years he devoted his genius to organizing the native tribes and to developing the gold and silver mines in southern Spain. Hamilcar's son, Hannibal, a boy nine years old, had accompanied his father to Spain. Before leaving Carthage, his father had led him to the altar and made him swear eternal hatred to the Roman race.

When twenty-six years old, *Hannibal* became commander-in-chief of the Carthaginian armies (220 B. C.) and at once began preparations for war with Rome. His first act was to attack the Greek city of Saguntum, which had for years been allied to Rome, and thus precipitated hostilities with the hated republic. Then assembling an army of 90,000 foot, 12,000 horse, and thirty-seven elephants, he committed the government of Spain to his brother, Hasdrubal, and marched towards the Alps, determined to carry the war into Italy.

When he reached the Rhone he found a large army of Gauls drawn up on the opposite bank to dispute his passage. This enemy was defeated by a skillful maneuvre. A detachment of troops was sent to cross the stream higher up, under cover of the night, with orders to attack the Gauls in the rear, on a signal being given. "Everything being prepared he began to cross the stream. The Gauls rushed down to oppose him, but soon saw their camp behind them in flames, and after a short resistance, turned and fled. The Roman army then crossed the Rhone "—*Goodrich*.

The elephants, dreading the water, could not be compelled to enter boats; they were, therefore, conveyed across by floats or rafts of timber covered with earth. "The animals, deceived by their appearance, took them for firm ground and suffered themselves to be led upon them."—*Goodrich*.

The great army now marched on up the valley of the

Rhone, obtaining supplies on the way from a Celtic chief, till sheer in front of them, loftier than the Pyrenees, rose the Alpine peaks. "Nature and man joined to oppose the passage." The tremendous height and steepness of the mountains, capped with snow, that seemed to rest among the clouds; the mountaineers, of barbarous and fierce aspect, dressed in skins, presented a scene that would have daunted a less bold and determined leader. Added to all these horrors "the season was now far advanced, it was October, and snow was falling on the higher portion of the trail." Hannibal seized the first pass at night while the mountaineers were resting. Thus gaining the advantage, the army pushed on up the steep ascent though often attacked by the hostile tribes who rolled down great rocks upon them from the precipices. "At times the crack of a whip would bring down an avalanche from the impending heights." In places the narrow way must be cut wider for the monstrous bodies of the elephants. Vast numbers of men, horses, and elephants were lost before the army escaped from these dangers. On the ninth day they reached the summit of the Alps, where they halted two days to rest. Here a great fall of snow, and the prospect of further difficulties, disheartened the soldiers; but Hannibal aroused them by the inspiring words, "Ye stand upon the Acropolis of Italy; yonder lies Rome."

With renewed spirits they commenced the toilsome descent. The difficulties now increased; the new-fallen snow had covered up the paths, and they lost their way. Along the edge of narrow precipices which went sheer down into unseen depths they had to creep with careful steps ; the least slip and none could save them. Often new roads must be cut with hands benumbed with cold.

Finally the path grew easier and the valleys more fertile. "Gradually from the land of everlasting snows they came down into the soft warmth of the Italian plains." "Fifteen days in all were spent in crossing the Alps; the route was probably the pass now known as Mont Cenis," though it has generally been said to be the Little St. Bernard.

This is the greatest march known in ancient times, but it was accomplished with a fearful sacrifice of life. "Of the fifty thousand and more with which Hannibal had begun the passage, barely half that number had survived the march, and these looked more like phantoms than men." Hannibal, however, was confident that he could gain the Gauls as auxiliaries, and in this he was not deceived. After recruiting his exhausted soldiers, he twice routed the Roman armies. He gained the goodwill of the Gauls by sparing their possessions and plundering only those of the Romans. They flocked to his standard and became a constant and reliable part of his army throughout his Italian campaigns.

The skillful generalship of Hannibal was constantly displayed, and the Roman consuls were no match for him. This fact was well illustrated in the battle of Trebia. The wily Carthaginian, knowing the impetuosity of the Romans, provoked them to a battle. It was a cold winter morning, and the Romans had been roused from their sleep to fight without having breakfasted. The Carthaginian cavalry, feigning a panic, fled to the river Trevia. The Romans pursued them across the stream, which was swollen by a heavy fall of rain. "The water was icy cold and almost up to their necks; they were hungry as well as chilled to the bone. They could not maintain their ground against fresh troops of the enemy, and were completely routed, the greater part of them perishing in the river and on its banks."

The following spring Hannibal led his army, now recruited by many Gauls, across the Apennines and southward through the flooded region of the Arno. Four days and three nights were consumed in wading through the marshes. The men suffered every hardship; Hannibal lost one of his eyes by acute inflammation, and, it was said, that his life was saved by his last remaining elephant. Notwithstanding these misfortunes he soon afterwards entrapped the Roman army in a mountain pass where they were bewildered by the fog and completely defeated. During this battle a dreadful earthquake occurred, which destroyed many cities, overturned mountains, and turned rivers from their courses; but such was the fury of the combatants that this great convulsion of nature passed unobserved.

"Rome was now saved by the prudence of Fabius, who was made dictator." "He saw that the only way of obtaining advantage over the enemy was by harrassing and fatiguing them without coming to a decisive battle." "Whenever they moved he watched their movements, straitened their quarters, and cut off their provisions. The soldiers began to murmur and called him *Cunctator* or 'the Delayer.' He was even accused of treachery, but nothing moved him from his course;

thus he gained time for the fitting out of new armaments."

By the next summer a large army had been raised, and disciplined, much superior to that of Hannibal, but commanded by two consuls who did not work well together. Varro, who had nothing to recommend him except wealth and self-conceit, gave the signal for battle without asking advice of his colleague. The Romans attempted to break through the center of the enemy's lines. Hannibal, observing this, ordered part of these troops to give way and allow the Romans to advance until they were surrounded. A chosen body of cavalry then fell upon their flanks and a horrible massacre occurred. Twenty-one tribunes, eighty senators, and from fifty to seventy thousand men were slain. This was the greatest defeat the Romans ever sustained. "Thousands of rings gathered from the hands of nobles who lay dead upon the field were sent as trophies to Carthage."

"The road lay open to Rome. 'Let me advance instantly with the horse,' urged the commander of the cavalry, 'and in four days thou shalt sup in the capitol.' Hannibal refused. 'Alas,' said the disappointed officer, 'thou knowest how to gain a victory, but not how to use one.'"—*Quackenbos*.

Great was the consternation at Rome. One-fifth of all the citizens able to bear arms had fallen in the disastrous campaign and every house was in mourning. In this hour of despair the senate stood calm and firm. Hannibal sent an embassy to offer terms of peace, the Senate would not permit the ambassadors to enter the gates. Hannibal withdrew his army to wealthy Capua, which opened its gates without resistance and became the winter quarters of the army. Southern Italy generally declared for the victor and Macedon and Syracuse also joined the Carthaginian, but the Latin cities never swerved for a moment from their loyalty.

The Roman Empire in Italy stood firm as a rock, and, maintaining war not only in Italy but in Spain, began slowly to win back what it had lost.

Siege of Syracuse.—After a siege of eight months Syracuse was captured by the Romans under Marcellus. It had been defended chiefly by the ingenuity of the famous mathematician, Archimedes. "He contrived stupendous engines which discharged masses of stone, and huge iron grapples that seized the Roman ships when they approached the walls, raised them in the air, and dashed them into the water. He is also said to have set fire to the hostile fleet by means of mirrors, and so terrified the Romans with his machines that at the sight of a rope or a stick on the walls they fled in dismay." —*Quackenbos*.

At length, during a festival of Diana, the city was taken (212 B. C.) and given up to pillage. Treasures of Grecian art, paintings and sculpture, which adorned this famous colony of ancient Hellas, were now removed to Rome. During the confusion of the pillage Archimedes perished. "He was engaged in study, when a Roman soldier rushed upon him and bade him follow to Marcellus. 'Wait,' said the Philosopher, 'till I have finished this problem'; whereupon the soldier, incensed at the delay, drew his sword and killed him." Syracuse never recovered from the blow inflicted upon her at this time by the relentless Romans.

Close of the war.—Meanwhile their luxurious city quarters were enervating the soldiers of Hannibal, and when called again into the field they were no longer equal to the fatigues of the war.

Before the fall of Syracuse the Romans laid siege to Capua. Hannibal hastened to the relief of the city, but not succeeding in breaking the lines of the besiegers he attempted to frighten them away by making a bold dash on Rome. In this he was disappointed, for the city was provided with defenders. It is said that Hannibal rode up to the very walls and discharged a javelin into the city. Fearing to undertake the siege of Rome, he retreated into Southern Italy, leaving Capua to her fate. It was soon taken and "paid the penalty that Rome never failed to inflict on an unfaithful ally." Its chief citizens were put to death, and great numbers of the inhabitants sold as slaves. The city was reduced to the rank of a village, being deprived of all political rights.

In the year following, Tarentum was taken and, as a last resource, Hannibal looked eagerly for assistance from his brother in Spain. Here Hasdrubal had defeated and killed two Roman generals, and then leaving the conduct of the war to others, followed about the same route formerly taken by Hannibal.

In 207 B. C. he descended the Alps upon the plain of Northern Italy, while Hannibal moved northward to meet him. "But the junction was never effected, for Hasdrubal's army was cut to pieces and its leader slain. His disfigured head flung into the camp was brought to

Hannibal, who cried out on beholding it, 'Ah! Carthage, I see thy doom.'"—*Quackenbos.*

"Somewhat later the Romans sent an army into Africa, and Hannibal (after an absence of nineteen years, fifteen of which were occupied in Italy) was recalled to defend his country from Scipio, but without success. The battle of Zama, 202 B. C. (see Allen's history) annihilated the last hope of Carthage, and forced her to submit to a disgraceful peace. Thus ended the second Punic war. In honor of his great victories, Scipio was surnamed Africanus."—*Quackenbos.*

Death of Hannibal.—Hannibal now proved himself as capable in the field of administration as in the conduct of war. "The reforms instituted by him in his native city enabled his countrymen not only to pay the indemnity demanded by the Romans but rapidly to regain their former prosperity."—*Allen.* The Romans, beholding his work with jealous eye, demanded his surrender. He fled to the court of Antiochus, who ruled the kingdom from the Ægean sea beyond the Tigris. When that king submitted to the Romans he sought refuge in an adjoining country. Still finding himself pursued by the vindictive Romans he ended his life by taking poison which he carried in a hollow ring. Thus perished one of the greatest captains of antiquity in the sixty-eighth year of his life (183 B. C.).

Third Punic war.—In a little more than half a century Rome, by successful campaigns in Greece and Asia Minor, had obtained her *first Asiatic province* of *Pergamus*, as well as the provinces of *Greece* and *Macedonia*. (See Grecian history.) The same year that saw the fall of *Corinth* witnessed also the destruction of *Carthage.* This city had again become wealthy and prosperous. Ships crowded her harbors and the country for miles around was a beautiful garden. The jealousy of Rome was aroused. Marcus Cato was sent as an ambassador to Africa, and on his return he is said to have presented a bunch of figs to the senate, saying "They are yet fresh. They came from Carthage. So near to us are our enemies, *Delenda est Carthago!*" (Carthage must be destroyed.)

The senate at last was moved by the constant denunciations of Cato, who never rose to speak or vote on any subject without adding the words, "I also think that Carthage should be destroyed." They soon found a pretext and issued a decree for the destruction of Carthage, permitting the inhabitants to build another city not nearer to the sea than ten miles.

"This was too much, even for a conquered people; they preferred a hopeless resistance. All classes labored incessantly to strengthen the fortifications of the city; prisoners were set free, and their chains forged into weapons; statues, vases—even gold and silver—were melted down for the same purpose, and the women braided their flowing locks into bow-strings."—*Quackenbos.* (Their arms and military stores had a short time before been surrendered to the Romans.)

In spite of these efforts, Scipio, the adopted son of Scipio Africanus, took the city after a three-years' siege, and burned it to the ground. A plough was driven over the site and a dreadful curse invoked upon any one who should attempt to rebuild it. The territory possessed by

"Carthage at the time of its fall was made the province of Africa, with Utica as its capital."

Scipio, surveying the ruins of the city he had conquered, could not refrain from tears. The thought that such might some time be the fate of his own city came to his mind, and he sadly repeated the words of Homer:

> "Yet come it will, the day decreed by fate,
> The day when thou, imperial Troy, must bend,
> And see thy warriors fall, thy glories end."

(See character of Scipio. Page 144, Myers.)

Decay of the Republic.—The Roman power by means of two or more centuries of conquest had obtained possession first of Italy, then of nearly all the countries bordering on the Mediterranean. The Roman Republic was now "mistress of the civilized world," but she had reached the summit of her greatness. She became proud and cruel. Her unjust wars for the sake of glory robbed her of her old time virtue, which had been her strength.

The provinces were the principal source of corruption. The revenues extorted from them were enough to support Rome in idleness. The people of the provinces had no redress from the cruelties practiced upon them, for their own courts of justice had no authority over their conquerors. It is related that Flaminius, when commanding an army in Cisalpine Gaul, caused a noble Gaul to be beheaded for the amusement of his favorite officers. The man was guilty of no offense, but the pleasing spectacle of his death was to compensate for the gladiatorial shows at Rome which they had missed. Flaminius was removed from the senate by the censors, but the courts had no power to punish him.

Cato was known for the severity with which he discharged his duty as censor of the public morals. For nearly half a century he was the leading politician of Rome. He contended against luxurious living and debasement of character and set an example by the purity and simplicity of his own life. Though he was a model in personal integrity, energy, and ability in war and in statesmanship, he was devoid of generosity and nobility of character. The indirect influence of his teachings was to emphasize what was selfish and ungenerous in Roman policy. It was he who urged the destruction of Carthage and the extension of the mischievous provincial system. He thought the degeneracy of character due to the fashionable Greek culture of the day. It must be admitted that the Greeks were not what they had been, and their art, literature, and philosophy at this age possessed no elevating or ennobling power. The doctrines of the Greek Epicurus were eagerly embraced by the Romans of the empire. Epicurus said: "Be virtuous because virtue will bring the greatest amount of happiness." The disciples of this corrupt age carried the teachings of their master to an excess he would have been first to condemn. Their whole philosophy was expressed in the proverb: "Let us eat, drink, and be merry, for tomorrow we die."

"As a result of the many wars, slaves had multiplied to an alarming extent. Numbers of these were trained as gladiators. Others cultivated the public lands, while the poor freeman could scarcely make a living."— *Quackenbos*. The simple peasant no longer cultivated his small farm. When Hannibal swept through the country with fire and sword he destroyed all these rural homes and reduced great districts to a condition where they fell an easy prey to speculators. These wealthy land-owners had transformed Italy into a country of great landed estates cultivated by slaves. As free labor can never exist by the side of slave labor, the peasants flocked to the city to be fed, amused, and humored by office-seekers who wished their votes. It was customary for a candidate to amuse the people with costly games and the governors of provinces kept the Roman populace in good humor by sending back gifts of grain. There was no substantial industry or commerce as at the present time, and no means were taken to enlighten and refine the community by science, literature, or religion. It is no wonder that they sank into a mere mob that threatened the destruction of their country.

A great change had also taken place in the army. The soldier no longer retired to his little farm when he had fought his country's battles, but was a soldier by profession. He fought for plunder and glory, not for love of country and for the protection of his own fireside.

The days of Fabricius were forgotten; presents from foreign kings were now received at Rome and generals and statesmen demanded money everywhere. The Romans became cruel and unjust, thus bringing about a century of civil strife which ended the republic. Nevertheless six great names were connected with the ensuing centuries; and, through the influence of those great leaders, the earliest years of the empire became the palmiest in Roman history. These names are: The

Gracchi, Marius, Cicero, Cæsar and Octavian.—*Adopted from Allen, Barnes and Myers.*

THE CIVIL WARS.

The Reforms of the Grac'chi.—Moved by the distress that prevailed among the lower classes, Tiberius and Caius Gracchus became noted champions in the cause of the people. They were grandsons of Scipio Africanus, and had been carefully and wisely brought up by their mother, Cornelia, a noble Roman lady. She had refused an offer of marriage with the king of Egypt in order that she might devote herself to the education of her sons.

The following story is a familiar one to all readers of history:

A rich lady friend was once exhibiting to Cornelia a casket of rare gems. When asked what her jewels were, the mother called in her two sons, saying, "These are my jewels."

The Gracchi, as they were called, became the most popular orators that Rome ever produced. They boldly proclaimed the rights of the people.

Tiberius first became tribune and secured the passage of a law directing the division of the public lands into homesteads for the needy. Attalus, king of Pergamus, a country in Asia Minor, bequeathed his vast riches to the Roman people. Tiberius proposed that, as the poorer classes had just been allotted small portions of land, the money should be divided amongst them, in order that they might stock their farms and build houses. "Before this plan could be carried out, his year of office expired, and unwilling to see the good he had begun left unfinished, he offered himself for ré-election, though this was contrary to law."—*Mary Ford*. On the day when the election was held, the nobles aroused a mob, who attacked Tiberius and his friends. There in the Roman Forum he and three hundred of his followers were killed and their bodies thrown into the Tiber. Never before had the forum been disgraced by such a scene of violence and bloodshed.

The fate of his brother Tiberius did not prevent *Caius Gracchus* from pursuing a similar course in the interest of the people. The Senate, fearing him, had appointed him magistrate in Sardinia for three years. Returning to Rome before that time he was summoned before the Senate to be publicly rebuked and expelled; "but he appealed to the people in a stirring speech. Caius had given years of study to attain perfection in the art of oratory; indeed, he was so careful in the modulation of his voice that a slave, standing behind him with a flute, gave him the proper note on which to begin, and the result was soon seen in the effect he produced on his audiences. The people were charmed with his eloquence, and when he put himself up for election as tribune, they thronged in such numbers to vote for him that even the house-tops were crowded. His brother Tiberius had been very dear to him, and in all his speeches he bitterly reproached the plebeians for allowing him to be slain."—*Mary Ford*.

Caius was chosen tribune in 123 B. C. He was particularly anxious for the distribution of the public lands and the sale of corn at a low price among the poor. The latter was a very unwise measure, for it was not long before the people were living in vicious indolence and feeding at the public expense. As the public lands of Italy had been mostly taken up, he proposed to establish twelve colonies in the provinces, and himself carried a body of settlers to the abandoned site of Carthage.

Other measures favored by Caius were bitterly opposed by the nobles, and the influence of Gracchus depending upon the support of a fickle people, he lost his election and became a private citizen. Such an intense excitement occurred when the senate attempted to repeal the laws that Caius had made that the two parties came into collision. Caius sought death at the hands of a faithful slave to prevent capture by his enemies.

"Cornelia survived her sons for many years. When she died, her early hope was fulfilled, and on the bronze statue raised to her memory in the forum were carved the words: 'Cornelia, the mother of the Gracchi.'"— *Mary Ford.*

With the Gracchi perished the real freedom of the republic, henceforth the power of the state was wielded by a corrupt and insolent aristocracy.

Marius and Sulla.—Soon after the death of Gracchi there arose two Roman leaders named Marius and Sulla. "They were ambitious not for the welfare of their fellow-men, and for right, honor, and noble deeds, but for themselves."

Sulla was a patrician and Marius was a representative of the plebeians. Marius was the son of a poor villager and passed his early life in the labors of the field. " His manners were boorish, his countenance frightful and his stature gigantic; his only virtue appears to have been personal bravery and military talent." Sulla on the contrary was "elegant, refined, and accomplished to the finger tips," and though younger than Marius soon became his rival in military exploits. In the war with Jugurtha, a prince who had taken violent possession of all Numidia, on the northern coast of Africa, Marius was consul and conducted the campaign; Sulla was a young officer under his command.

By his own desire Sulla was sent on a dangerous errand to accomplish the treacherous seizure of Jugurtha. His success in this attempt emboldened him to claim himself as victor and to have a ring made representing Jugurtha's surrender to him, though the Consul Marius received all the honors at Rome. Henceforth Marius and Sulla were bitter rivals.—*Adapted from Butterworth, Goodrich, Mary Ford, Allen, and Myers.*

The Cimbri and Teutones.—(113–110 B. C.)—While half of the Roman army was in Africa, an invasion from the barbaric tribes of the north swept over the new province of Transalpine Gaul and threatened Italy. Two German tribes called the Cimbri and Teutones had left their forests and were seeking new homes in the south. They traveled in wagons, bringing with them their property, wives, and children. The Celtic tribes were no match for this multitude of gigantic savages and fled before them as they advanced. Several Roman armies were cut to pieces in Gaul and the senate in despair appealed to Caius Marius as the only man who could save the state. For two or three successive years, while the victorious Germans roamed through Gaul and Spain, Marius was again and again reinstated consul. It was contrary to law but the safety of the state demanded it.

At last the invaders again set their faces towards Italy, and Marius, accompanied by Sulla, as one of his most skillful lieutenants, hastened into northern Italy. The barbarians having divided, he hurried over the Alps, met the Teutons not far from Marseilles and almost annihilated the entire host. The Cimbri, in the meantime, had entered Italy by the eastern Alps and were ravaging the rich plains of the Po. They were met the following year, 101 B. C., by Marius and his colleague. The lines of the barbarians were drawn up in a body nearly three miles square, the men of the outer ranks being linked together by chains passed through their belts. This proved their ruin, for the Romans hewed their way through to the wagons, which were placed in the center. There the women, assisted by the dogs, fought as desperately as the men, but were soon overpowered by the trained legions. None could escape and the few who survived were sold as slaves in the Roman markets. Great were the rejoicings at Rome over these two great victories, and Marius was hailed as " Savior of his country " and " third founder of the city." For the present, indeed, Rome was saved, but this horde of barbarians that had been slaughtered was but the vanguard of those northern hosts that, five hundred years later, spread desolation throughout the empire and broke it into fragments.—*Adapted.*

Servile and Social Wars.—The popularity of Marius was now at its height, and five times running he was elected consul. Scarcely was the war with the barbarians at an end, before a second uprising of the slaves took place in Sicily. As before, the slaves chose a fortune-teller for their leader. The rebellion was soon crushed, and a number of the slaves were brought to fight as gladiators in the Roman theatre; there, one by one, they killed each other, till the last man fell upon his own sword.

"Marius now put himself up for election as consul for the sixth time, and there being no necessity for this illegal proceeding, the people suspected him of wanting to get all the power of the state into his own hands, and his popularity began to decline."—*Mary Ford.*

The important question at Rome was now that of the Italian allies, who were more and more impatient to obtain Roman citizenship. At last, when hopeless of success by legislation, the Italians attempted to gain their rights by violence. This contest, called the Social War, was kept up for two years, with successes on both sides. "Marius obtained two great victories over the others, though his soldiers fought very unwillingly, recognizing in the opposite ranks many of their own friends and kinsmen."—*Mary Ford.*

After thousands of lives had been sacrificed and plantations laid waste the senate granted what it had so churlishly refused at the begining of the war, namely, the citizenship of the Italian states. At a later time, in the days of the empire, this franchise was extended to all the free inhabitants of the provinces beyond the confines of Italy.

First Mithridatic War.—Just before the close of the

social war, news came to Rome that Mithrida'tes the Great, king of Pontus, had proclaimed himself deliverer of Asia Minor from the Roman yoke. The Romans appointed Sulla to conduct the war against the king. Marius was very angry, and by unscrupulous means managed to wrest the command from his rival. Sulla now led his legions to Rome, and, for the first time since the founding of Rome, civil war existed within the walls of the city.

Marius, deserted by a large number of his men, was obliged to take to flight. After many adventures he at last crossed the Mediterranean and reached the ruins of Carthage. "Here he lived in a hut. He was an old man now—over seventy years old—and one would have thought that his exile would have softened his heart and led him to long for the virtues that bring peace to the soul. He once said to a messenger from Rome, 'Go tell your master that you have seen Caius Marius sitting an exile amid the ruins of Carthage.'"—*Butterworth.*

"Meanwhile Sulla's career in the East was a series of victories. Athens, which had revolted to Mithrida'tes, was taken by storm. Greece and Asia Minor were conquered, and the king submitted to a humiliating peace."—*Quackenbos.*

Return of Marius.—After Sulla's departure Marius was recalled from exile by his friends at Rome. He now took a fearful revenge for all he had suffered. He closed the gates of the city and caused all whom he considered his enemies to be slaughtered. "Finally, the monster had himself declared consul for the seventh time." "Was he happy? Amid his cruel triumph he fell sick. His sufferings were terrible. He imagined himself Sulla, and at the head of the army in Asia. 'Mithridates!' he was heard to cry. He shouted orders to the imaginary army of Sulla, and so warring in his dreams he became exhausted by frenzy, and sunk into the sleep of death."—*Butterworth.*

Return of Sulla.—Sulla returned and soon all Italy lay prostrate before him. The plebeians and friends of Marius now had cause for fear. Again the streets of Rome ran red with blood. "The massacres of Marius, however, were kind and gentle compared with the proscriptions of Sulla; every day he published new lists of those condemned to die, until the number of victims could be reckoned by thousands."—*Mary Ford.* "The possession of property was a sufficient offense. 'Alas!' exclaimed one who read his name among the doomed, 'my villa is my destruction.' Even whole states of Italy which had sided with Marius were depopulated to make room for colonies of Sulla's legions."—*Quackenbos.*

"When Sulla had taken possession of the supreme power in Rome, and was looking over the list of public men, in order to arrange a new system of government, his eye met a name which caused him to hesitate. It was **Julius Cæsar.** He was born July 12, 100 B. C."—*Butterworth.*

"It was a name of destiny. Julius Cæsar was to conquer the world for Rome, and Rome for himself, and well might Sulla pause at that name. Cæsar was a young man then. He was a patrician by birth, a descendant from a long line of noble families, related by marriage to Marius. Though a patrician, his heart had turned to the popular party.

"Sulla was about to place Cæsar's name on the proscribed list, when his many powerful friends interceded in his behalf. Sulla suspended judgment, but ordered Cæsar to give up his wife, who was a daughter of Cinna, a partisan of Marius.

"Cæsar refused to be false to his wife and friends, and fled from the city. Then Sulla proscribed him, and deprived him of his offices and titles, and treated him as one of the enemies of Rome."

"Cæsar had studied Greek, and was a master of rhetoric and history. His heart was given to the preparation for a public career. In his exile he went to Rhodes, where he met a former preceptor, and continued his studies, wishing to become a master of oratory. Sulla died, and Cæsar cautiously returned to Rome."—*Butterworth.*

(See description of forum, "Little Arthur's History of Rome," page 102.)

"He appeared in the forum as an orator and a champion of the people. His oratory carried the popular feeling; he soon found himself a hero, and his power grew. Here Cæsar delivered two funeral orations over members of his own family, and in them pleaded the cause of the rights of the people.

"He was elected to office, and he rose from one position of influence to another, until he was made quæstor, and was finally elected consul.

"His rise was not altogether honorable. He spent his wealth in entertainments and public shows, to influence the people for political ends. He studied the art of pleasing the people for his own advancement. But he was a patrician who had espoused the cause of the people, and for this reason he became the idol of Rome. Wherever he went, the streets shouted; wherever he sat down, he was the head of the festal table. His ambition grew; like Alexander, he must have the earth—nothing less would content him.—*Adapted.*

"But before we go further, we must tell you something in regard to his great rival, Pompey. This hero conquered the East, while Cæsar subdued the West. (To be continued.)—*Butterworth.*

Pompey the Great.—"Caius Pompeius Magnus, or Pompey the Great, was born 106 B. C. He was a partisan of Sulla and was bred to the life of a soldier. He took a prominent part in the civil wars, and, becoming a popular hero, was elected consul. He left the aristocratic party and became a leader and voice of the people.

"In 67-66 he drove the pirates from the Mediterranean; in 65-62 he conquered Mithridates, and Antiochus, king of Syria. He subdued the Jewish nation, captured Jerusalem, entered the Holy of Holies in the Jewish temple, and made Palestine a province of Rome. He entered Rome in triumph in 61 B. C. He became a friend of Cæsar, and the united heroes joined with them in their political schemes, Crassus, a man of great wealth and influence in Rome. The three were called the First Triumvirate."—*Butterworth.*

Julius Cæsar (Continued).—Cæsar's first province was Spain. Before going to take possession of it, he was obliged to apply to Crassus to satisfy those creditors who were most uneasy and would not be put off any longer. In his journey, as he was crossing the Alps and passing by a small village of the barbarians, with but few inhabitants and those wretchedly poor, he remarked, "For my part, I had rather be the first man among these fellows than the second man in Rome."

The military life of this wonderful commander had at last begun, when he was forty years old. His friends once found him in tears while reading the history of Alexander. When asked why he wept, he said, "Do you think I have not just cause to weep when I consider that Alexander, at my age, had conquered so many nations, and I have, all this time, done nothing that is memorable."

Cæsar found Spain in a very rebellious state, but with great energy and skill he soon reduced it to submission and established a just and firm rule. "By this wise management he was able to leave his province with a fair reputation; being rich himself and having enriched his soldiers and received from them the honorable name of Imperator."

In less than a year he returned to Rome, and, being doubly supported by Pompey and Crassus, was promoted to the consulship.

The days of Roman liberty were now at an end. Henceforth the government was in the hands of ambitious leaders. Three great men were now at the head of affairs in Rome—Cæsar, Pompey, and Crassus. Cæsar was, however, the master as well of the senate as of the people. By his influence, an agrarian law was passed, for the division of some public lands among the poorer citizens. The best and most honorable of the senators opposed it, but this gave him a pretext to appeal to the people and convince them of his devotion to their cause. Everything now gave way to Cæsar; even Cicero, whose opposition they feared, was banished. (See stories of Cato and Cicero, "Little Arthur's History of Rome.") Cæsar's desire now was to have an army at his command; this he obtained, being appointed to the charge of the provinces of Gaul, both Cisalpine and Transalpine, for five years.—*Adapted from Plutarch, Goodrich, and Allen.*

Physical Gaul.—Gaul (Gallia) was the name given by the ancients to that country which extended from the Pyrenees to the Alps and the Rhine, embracing modern France and Belgium, with part of Holland and Switzerland and a small part of Germany.

The surface of France exhibits, in general, an advantageous succession of highland and lowland. Less level than Poland, northern Germany, and European Russia, it is on the whole less mountainous than Spain and Italy, and may with great propriety be compared with England. In France the mountainous districts are in the south and east, and may be said to be to that country what Wales and Scotland are to Great Britain.

The region in which the olive tree is cultivated is limited by a line from the Garonne to Lyons, on the Rhone; the region of the vine from the mouth of the Loire to Sedan; and the northern region is characterized by the apple tree.

The cultivation of grain has always been the chief business of French agriculturists. The quantity of wheat produced in France, large as it is, does not at present meet the wants of the population, and great quantities are every day imported from Russia, Prussia, Roumania, Egypt, and America.

France is but inadequately supplied with harbors, her long tract of coast, washed by the Atlantic and the Bay of Biscay, has scarcely three or four good seaports, and those on the southern shore of the channel form a striking contrast to the spacious inlets on the English side. Cal'ais, one of the best harbors in the north, is not to be compared with Dover. Le Havre De Grace, at the mouth of the Seine, is the best mercantile harbor in the north of France. Brest, in Brittany, is the great maritime port on the Atlantic for the navy. Bordeaux is situated on the Garonne, where the river is nearly equal in width to the Thames in London. Nantes, at the mouth of the Loire, is now connected with Liverpool by a regular service of steamers. On the Mediterranean, France has the ports of Marseilles, the most spacious and secure on the coast, Nice, and the great maritime port, arsenal and dock-yard of Toulon.—*Compiled from Britannica.*

Ancient People of Gaul.—"The history of France may well begin with the words which open Cæsar's famous chronicle: 'Gaul is divided into three parts.' The southwest part was inhabited by a people of darker complexion, less sociable, less bright, and not of Aryan race. The descendants of these people still dwell amid the fastnesses of the Pyrenees, in the Basque provinces of Spain, and differ alike from the Spaniards and Frenchmen. In the north, some German tribes had crossed the Rhine, but with these exceptions the inhabitants were of the Celtic race, called Celts or Gauls."—*Britannica.*

Description of Ancient Gauls.—(See p. 371, Barnes.)

Cæsar Enters Gaul.—At the time Cæsar was appointed governor of Gaul, the Romans had possession of the colony of Nar'bonen'sis, the territory between the Pyrenees and the Alps, except that which belonged to the Greek republic of Massilia. "West of the Rhone the province was separated from free Gaul by the Cevennes Mountains; east of these mountains the Rhone and its tributary, the Saône, afforded a direct passage into the heart of Europe. It was by this natural route that Cæsar advanced in his schemes of conquest."—*Allen.*

When Cæsar entered Gaul, he found the natives in a half-barbarous state, split up into about sixty clans, each with its elected chieftain, its Druids or priests, and its bodies of warriors or horsemen.

(See Life of Cæsar, Plutarch.)

Cæsar in Gaul.—Thus far we have followed Cæsar's actions before the war with Gaul. After this he seems to begin his course afresh, and to enter upon a new life and scene of action.

"His first war in Gaul was against the Helvetians, who inhabited modern Switzerland. Dissatisfied with their rugged country they burned their own towns, twelve in number, and four hundred villages, and proposed to migrate across the country to the shores of the Bay of Biscay. He considered their restlessness a menace to the Roman province of Gaul, and, consequently marched against them. These people were not inferior in courage to the Cimbri and Teutons. After a long and severe combat he drove the main army out of the field, but found the hardest work at their carriages and ramparts, where not only the men stood and fought, but the women, also, and children, defended themselves till they were cut to pieces. Gathering together those who had escaped out of the battle he obliged them to re-occupy the country which they had deserted and the cities which they had burned. This he did for fear the Germans should pass it and possess themselves of the land while it lay uninhabited.

"His second war was in defense of the Gauls against the Germans. But, finding his officers timorous, Cæsar called them together and advised them to march off, and not run the hazard of a battle against their inclinations, since they had such weak and unmanly feelings. 'I will take only the tenth legion and march against the barbarians whom I do not expect to find more formidable than the Cimbri, nor shall they find me a general inferior to Marius.' Upon this the tenth legion sent their acknowledgments and thanks, and the other legions blamed their officers, with great vigor and zeal, followed him many days' journey till they encamped within two hundred furlongs of the enemy."
—*Plutarch*.

The defeat of these Germans under Ariovistus, which soon took place, was an event of great moment in the history of the world, for by it the onward movement of the Germans was arrested, and held in check for nearly five hundred years. "After this action Cæsar left his army at their winter quarters in Gaul, and, in order to attend to affairs at Rome, stationed himself in Cisalpine Gaul, in the valley of the Po. There he sat down and employed himself in courting the favor of the people; great numbers coming to him continually, and always finding their requests answered; for he never failed to dismiss all with pleasant pledges of his kindness in hand, and further hopes for the future."

Narrow Escape in the Belgian Forests.—(See Plutarch.)

Conquests in Germany and Britain.—"Cæsar was ambitious of the honor of being the first man that should pass the Rhine with an army. Early in the spring of 55 B. C., he constructed a bridge across the Rhine and led his legions against the Germans in their native woods and swamps." When he had burned the enemies' country, and encouraged those who embraced the Roman interest, he went back into Gaul, after eighteen days' stay in Germany. But his expedition into Britain was the most famous testimony of his courage. For he was the first who brought a navy into the western ocean or who sailed into the Atlantic with an army to make war; and by invading an island whose existence was even questioned at that time, he might be said to have carried the Roman Empire beyond the limits of the known world. He passed thither twice from that part of Gaul which lies over against it, and in several battles which he fought did more hurt to the enemy than service to himself, for the islanders were so miserably poor that they had nothing worth being plundered of. When he found himself unable to put such an end to the war as he wished, he was content to take hostages from the king,

and to impose a tribute, and then quitted the island."—
Plutarch.

Character of Cæsar.—"The period of the conquest of Gaul and Britain shows Cæsar to have been a soldier and general not the least inferior to any of the greatest and most admired commanders who had ever appeared at the head of armies.

"Such was the affection of his soldiers, and their attachment to his person, that they, who, under other commanders, were nothing above the common rate of men, became invincible when Cæsar's glory was concerned, and met the most dreadful dangers with a courage which nothing could resist.

"This courage, and this great ambition, were cultivated and cherished, in the first place, by the generous manner in which Cæsar rewarded his troops, and the honors which he paid them. His whole conduct showed that he did not accumulate riches to minister to luxury, or to serve any pleasures of his own, but that he considered himself no farther rich than he was in a condition to do justice to the merit of his soldiers.

"Another thing that contributed to make them invincible was their seeing Cæsar always take his share of the danger, and never desire any exemption from labor and fatigue. As for his exposing his person to danger, they were not surprised, for they knew his passion for glory, but they were astonished at his patience under toil, so far, in all appearance, above his bodily powers, for he was of a slender make, fair, of a delicate constitution, and subject to violent headaches and epileptic fits. He did not, however, make these disorders a pretense for indulging himself. On the contrary, he sought in war a remedy for his infirmities, endeavoring to strengthen his constitution by long marches, by simple diet, by seldom coming under cover. Thus he contended against his distemper, and fortified himself against its attacks.

"When he slept it was commonly upon a march, either in a chariot or a litter, that rest might be no hindrance to the business. In daytime he visited the castles, cities, and fortified camps with a servant at his side, and with a soldier behind who carried his sword. He drove so rapidly that when he first left Rome he arrived at the river Rhone within eight days. He had been an expert rider from his childhood, for it was usual with him to sit with his hands joined behind his back, and so, to put his horse to its full speed. And in this war, he disciplined himself so far as to be able to dictate letters from on horseback, and to give directions to two who took notes at the same time, or as Oppius says, 'to more.'"

Thus he dictated his famous commentaries which furnish us a faithful and graphic account of his marches, battles, and sieges, besides being admired for their elegance and style.

"Cæsar remained nine years in Gaul. During that time he took eight hundred cities by assault, conquered three hundred nations, and fought pitched battles at different times with three million of men, one million of which he slaughtered and made another million prisoners."—*Plutarch*.

Result of Cæsar's Conquests.—"The newly conquered territory was divided into three districts, the northern, southwestern, and central, the latter of which took its name from the city at the junction of the Rhone and Saône, Lugdu'um (Lyons). The conquest of Gaul was perhaps the most important the Romans had yet made outside of their natural boundaries. It was not a large source of revenue, and that was well, but it was a broad, fertile land, occupied by a people who readily adopted Roman institutions and civilization, and who speedily became Romanized. Gaul became a seat of flourishing trade and of well-conducted schools. Its situation, giving access at once to Britain and to Germany, made it, in the latter empire, the center of civilization and power in Western Europe."—*Allen.*

Rivalry between Cæsar and Pompey. — "Cæsar had long ago resolved upon the overthrow of Pompey as had Pompey upon his. For Crassus, the fear of whom had hitherto kept them in peace, having now been killed in Parthia, the one who wished to make himself the greatest man in Rome had only to overthrow the other."— *Plutarch.* "Cæsar became more and more a favorite of the people and Pompey went over to the patrician or aristocratic party, and endeavored to deprive Cæsar of his offices and honors."—*Butterworth.* (See Myers.)

"The senate, coming under the influence of the peace party, ordered both Cæsar and Pompey to lay down arms. Cæsar declared that he was ready to do this, if Pompey would do the same; but Pompey stubbornly refused." The next year the war party ordered Cæsar to give up his command. Mark Antony and Cassius, who supported Cæsar, were driven from the senate. They fled to Cæsar's camp, in Cisalpine Gaul, and demanded protection."—*Allen.*

March upon Rome.—"Cæsar at once marched upon Rome. 'The die is cast.' So Cæsar is reported to have said on crossing the Rubicon. The river was in Cisalpine Gaul, on the boundary of the Roman Empire. Cæsar crossed the stream in disobedience to the senate, and to the Roman law, which forbade a general to approach Rome with his army, after a foreign war, except when invited to a triumph. The Rubicon was a small stream, and the territory around it of little worth; but when Cæsar crossed the boundary, the Roman republic fell, after an existence of nearly five hundred years."—*Butterworth.*

"Cæsar's prompt action threw his opponents into distraction and panic. Though Pompey had boasted that with one stamp of his foot, an army would spring from the ground, he now fled to Greece without striking a blow. In sixty days, Cæsar made himself master of all Italy without bloodshed. He was made dictator and the ambitious dreams of his youth seemed fulfilled."—*Butterworth.*

Before following his enemy into the East, Cæsar brought Italy, Gaul, and Spain under his authority. He also procured the passage of an important act giving the citizenship to the inhabitants of Cisalpine Gaul.

"Cæsar with a small army now crossed the sea to meet Pompey. His soldiers were so full of faith in the destiny of their leader, and so confident of victory, that no ordinary force could withstand them.

"'Friends,' said Cæsar, on the stormy waters, as he

went before his little army, one dark windy night, on a slender ship—'friends, you have nothing to fear. You are carrying Cæsar!'"—*Butterworth.*

Conquest of Pompey.—"The two armies met on the plain of Pharsalia. Pompey had the larger army, Cæsar had better trained legions. Each felt certain of victory. The disciplined legions of Cæsar were soon masters of the field. Pompey fled from the red field to his camp, and sunk down in his tent a ruined man. His star had set after thirty years. The soldiers of Cæsar appeared before his tent, and he mounted his horse and fled again. He sought refuge in Egypt, in the land of the Ptolemies. There he was assassinated by the friends of Cæsar, and his body was burned on a funeral pyre. His dissevered head was the first sight that greeted Cæsar when he arrived at Alexandria in pursuit."—*Butterworth.*

It is said that Cæsar wept bitter tears, and directed that an honorable burial be given to the remains.

Other Conquests.—A few months were spent by Cæsar in ordering affairs in Egypt, where he restored Cleopatra to her throne and suppressed a dangerous revolt. He then marched into Asia against the son of Mithridates. The speedy overthrow of this prince he announced in the brief sentence, "*Veni, vidi, vici*" ("I came, I saw, I conquered").

Cato and other republican leaders had assembled a great force in Africa, whereupon Cæsar hurried his conquering legions forward and a decisive battle was fought (B. C. 46) fatal to the republic.

(See Life of Cato, "Little Arthur's History of Rome.")

Cæsar's Triumph.—On his return to Rome Cæsar celebrated a four-days' triumph for his victories in Gaul, Egypt, and Asia; patriotism was still too strong in the Roman mind to permit him a triumph over fellow-citizens.

"In the triumphal procession were led captive princes from all parts of the world. Beneath his standards marched soldiers gathered out of almost every country beneath the heavens. Seventy-five million dollars of treasure were displayed. Splendid games and tables attested the liberality of the conqueror. Sixty thousand couches were set for the multitudes. The shows of the theater and the combats of the arena followed one another in an endless round.

"The senate made Cæsar perpetual dictator, and conferred upon him the powers of censor, consul, and tribune, with the title of Pontifex Maximus and Imperator (whence emperor). He was to sit in a golden chair in the senate-house, and his statue was placed in the capitol opposite to that of Jupiter."—*Myers.*

Cæsar's Government.—Cæsar now showed as great ability as a statesman as he had before displayed as a soldier. Order and justice were restored, and great reforms projected. To gratify his army, he sent out colonies to all the different provinces, the most remarkable of which were those sent to rebuild Corinth and Carthage. The provinces were governed with greater wisdom, and some of them, including Gaul, were given Roman citizenship. Most important of all of his achievements was the revision of the calendar by the addition of the extra day of the leap year. This brought the festivals once more in their proper seasons. The calendar then formed is known as the Julian Calendar, and with some slight improvements is in use to-day. (See Barnes).

Cæsar's Assassination.—"But all the genius of Cæsar, and all the wisdom and clemency which marked his exercise of power, could not compensate in the minds of his countrymen for the crime of elevating himself on the ruins of the republic." It was rumored that he designed to assume the title of king, a name that was odious to the Roman people. At a festival Mark Antony offered him a crown. The murmurs of the multitude compelled him to refuse it, but he seemed to thrust it aside reluctantly. At length a conspiracy was formed for his destruction. Brutus and Cassius, the leaders, resolved to put the plot into execution in the senate-house, on the ides of March. "The augurs had foretold that this day would be fatal to Cæsar." His wife, Calpurnia, dreamed on the night previous that she saw him assassinated, and endeavored to detain him, but failed. On his way to the senate-house a paper was placed in his hands containing an account of the plot, but he gave it no attention.

As he entered the assembly chamber he recognized the soothsayer, and remarked to him, "The ides of March have come," to which he received the reply, "Yes, but not gone." "As soon as Cæsar had taken his place the conspirators approached under pretense of saluting him." At a given signal their daggers were drawn and they rushed upon him. He defended himself at first with great vigor, but seeing his loved and trusted Brutus among his assailants, he exclaimed, "*Et tu, Brute!*" (And thou, too, Brutus!) and, covering his face with his toga, sank dead at the foot of Pompey's statue.—*Compiled from Goodrich.*

Results.—The conspirators expected to be applauded by the people as liberators of their country, but they were doomed to disappointment. The senate rushed horror-stricken to their homes. The people were silent and their faces grew pale as they recalled the proscriptions of Sulla. Mark Antony, the trusted friend and secretary of Cæsar, planned a scheme for seizing upon the chief authority. He obtained possession of Cæsar's papers and money and upon the day set for the funeral ceremonies he delivered the usual funeral oration. "He first read them Cæsar's will, in which he made Octavius, his sister's grandson, his heir, permitting him to take the name of Cæsar with three-fourths of his private fortune. To the people of Rome were left the gardens he possessed on the other side of the Tiber, and to every citizen three hundred sesterces or about eleven dollars and a quarter."—*Goodrich.* He rehearsed the great deeds of Cæsar and the honor he had brought to the Roman name, and finally held up Cæsar's rent and bloody toga. The people excited by this artful eloquence could no longer restrain their indignation against the conspirtors. Brutus and Cassius sought refuge in Greece. The next year they were pursued and the issue decided on the field of Philippi. "Brutus and Cassius were defeated and, in despair, committed suicide." The Roman world was again in the hands of two masters, Antony in the East, and Octavius in the West.

Death of Antony and Cleopatra.—After a disgraceful career in Egypt Antony ended his life with his own hand. Cleopatra, the last of the Ptolemies was made captive; and, resolved not to be taken to Rome to grace the triumph of Octavius, she applied an asp to her arm, thus terminating her guilty career.

"Egypt now became a Roman province and the enormous wealth of that country was seized by Octavius and transported to Rome."

"Cæsar Octavius was now undisputed master of the civilized world." After his return to Italy the senate saluted him with the name of Augustus. "This title was at first only personal, but afterwards it was assumed by the Roman emperors on attaining the dignity of the purple."—*Goodrich*.

Establishment of the Empire.—The Senate had conferred upon Augustus the entire authority of the government, but he flattered the people by a show of republican forms. "To the Senate he gave the chief power in the administration of his government, while he secured the fidelity of the people and the army by donations and acts of favor. By these means he caused the odium of severity to fall upon the Senate, while the popularity of pardon was solely his own." "The various offices of state were continued, but he engrossed them all." "He was consul, tribune, censor, pontifex maximus (superintendent of religious matters), and imperator (commander-in-chief)." "Every ten years he went through the farce of laying down his rank as chief of the army." "The people believed themselves restored to their former freedom, and the Senate imagined their ancient power re-established."—*Goodrich*.

Rome Under Augustus.—"The architectural splendor of Rome properly dates from the reign of Augustus, who boasted that he 'found it of brick and left it in marble.' Among the chief ornamental structures was the capitol. This was built on the Capitoline Hill, the highest in the city, and was ascended from the forum by a flight of one hundred steps. The gates were of brass overlaid with gold, and the whole building was so plentifully adorned in this manner that it acquired the name of the 'Golden Capitol.' The Senate House was the grand legislative hall of the nation. It was decorated with the statues of eminent warriors and statesmen. The Pantheon, or temple of all the gods, built in the reign of Augustus by his son-in-law Agrippa, is now a Christian church, and is the best preserved ancient building in Rome. It is universally admired for its fine dome and portico." The noble form of the dome had been developed from the arch, the distinctive feature of Roman architecture.

"In the valley between the Palatine and Capitoline Hills was the forum, or place of public assembly, and great market. It was surrounded with halls for the administration of justice, temples, and public officers. It was also adorned with statues of eminent Romans, and various trophies from conquered nations. Among these memorials of conquest were several rostra or prows of ships, taken from the Carthaginians. These were used to ornament the pulpits from which the magistrates and public officers harangued the general assemblies of the people. Thus originated the phrase, 'to mount the rostrum.'

"The porticos or piazzas were very numerous at Rome; these were covered colonnades, adorned with statues, and were designed as places for the citizens to meet for business or walk for pleasure. The city was adorned with triumphal arches, having statues and various sculptured ornaments." Some of these were very magnificent, being built of the finest marble. The most noted of these monuments were built by Titus and Constantine, both of which are still standing. (See Myers and Barnes.)

"Augustus, himself, enumerated twelve temples which he had built, besides repairing eighty-two which had fallen to decay, and building or restoring aqueducts, theatres, and porticos." "The people were not taxed or oppressed any way for these improvements, which were made at the expense of Augustus himself and the wealthy nobles, who were stimulated by his example." "The works of Augustus were directed towards the general embellishment of the city, rather than the erection of any particular edifice; and the Campus Martius, till then an open space, began to be covered with elegant buildings; but there was no royal palace, for the emperor resided in a private house and his style of living was not different from that of the rich citizen." It is said that his toga was woven by his wife and her maidens.

"The city of Rome, during the prosperous days of the empire, contained four hundred and twenty temples, besides theaters, amphitheaters, circuses, and public baths of vast extent. Some of the baths were constructed of marble, and were sufficiently large to accommodate three thousand bathers at once. Aqueducts of enormous size conveyed a copious supply of water from the neighboring country into Rome, and kept in play a prodigious number of fountains, many of which were remarkable for their architectural beauty.

'Thirty-one great roads centered in Rome. Augustus erected a gift pillar in the middle of the forum, from which the distances on the various roads were reckoned. There were thirty gates to the city, and eight bridges crossed the Tiber."—*Goodrich.*

Roman Civilization was now spreading through the empire. Learning was cultivated to such an extent that this period of Roman literature is known as the "Golden Age of the Poets" or the "Augustan Age." "Augustus was a literary man, and his principal adviser, Mæcenas, was a lover of poetry and art. It was the ambition of the emperor to glorify Rome in history, poetry, and art, and he admitted to his friendship men of genius and literary tastes, however humble may have been their birth." —*Butterworth.* Every man of rank had a library, and among the many distinguished writers of this age were Horace, Virgil, Ovid, and Livy. (See Barnes and "Little Arthur's History of Rome.") The Latin language became the universal bond of intercourse throughout the empire, though the Greek still prevailed in the East.

" The books were made of sheets of papyrus pasted together in a length and rolled on a stick. The writing was in columns with a space between. These rolls, called volumes, were kept in cases in the libraries. There were many book-sellers at Rome, and most of them employed people to make copies of the books they had on sale, of which a list was usually hung up on the shop door.

"Wherever the Roman dominion was firmly established, many opulent families went to reside, and as they were the superior people, the natives of the higher classes adopted their dress, language, and manners. Villas and ornamental gardens were constructed, roads made, and the people taught many useful arts of which before they were ignorant.

"They greatly improved the *agriculture* and *horticulture* of Europe, by introducing into the provinces the flowers and fruits of the East, and the cultivation of flax from Egypt.

Manufactures.—"It was in the time of Augustus, when Egypt became a Roman province, that linen began to be used among the Romans, a manufacture for which the Egyptians were particularly famous. Glass was also manufactured at Alexandria, and sent to Rome, which was the greatest market at this period for the richest productions of every country. Many manufactures were carried on in various parts of Italy, the slaves doing the work. One of them was paper made from the papyrus of Europe. Tapestry was made at Padua, and steel goods of all kinds at Como."

Commerce.—"The Roman succeeded in Asia to the great commercial marts of the Phœnicians, Greeks, and Egyptians, and acquired in Africa the ancient trading stations of the Carthaginians. Yet they made little or no effort to encourage traffic, and opened no new routes for trade. The principal trade was in grain and other provisions for the use of the capital.

"The inhabitants of Rome were, generally speaking, plentifully supplied with the luxuries, as well as the necessaries, from different parts of the empire. Ice and excellent cheese were sent from the Alpine districts; pork, geese, and salt, in large quantities, from Gaul; spices, perfumes, and precious stones, from the East, as well as many beautiful manufactured articles; and they also received an abundance of gold, and silver, and iron, as tribute from various nations. Among the commodities obtained by the Romans from distant parts of the world was manufactured silk, which they purchased of a people who came to their eastern dominions from some unknown country beyond; but whether they were Tartars, Chinese, or Indians is uncertain.

" The Romans were totally unacquainted with the nature of silk. They did not know how or where it was produced; but they were willing to give any price for it because it was rare and beautiful. It was so scarce, that they made their slaves unweave the thick eastern silks, to manufacture slighter ones, so that they might have two or three yards for one.

"At this early period it was worn only by the ladies of the highest rank; but in the course of time, the fine gentlemen of Rome used silk in their attire either in the form of a toga, a scarf, or a loose kind of a robe; for it was about this time that the toga began to be left off." *Goodrich.*

Roman Customs.—(See Goodrich's Roman History and Barnes'.)

Judea and the Birth of Christ.—After the rule of Ptolemy, "the Jews found that their new rulers were not so kind as Alexander the Great had been, for they were ill-treated by them because they would not worship heathen gods. So bad did matters become that at last the city of Jerusalem was besieged and captured by the Greek king of Syria, the temple overthrown, and thousands of Jews killed. A brave family called the Maccabees, under the leadership of Judas, revolted against this governor. After several years of hard fighting, they got the mastery of the Greeks and rebuilt the temple. Later on, the High Priest, who was ruler of the nation, took the title of 'king.' Quarrels arose between different parties among themselves, which led to fighting, and some of them asked help of Rome against their brethren. Pompey came with an army to restore peace. Many priests were killed before the altar, and the High Priest was deprived of the title of 'king,' and lost much of his kingdom.

"Some years after, the temple was plundered by the Roman general, and, at last, an Edomite, by the name of Herod, was put on the ancient throne of David. This king was called 'The Great,' because of the splendid buildings he ordered to be made, one of which was the magnificent temple where Jesus walked and talked. It was much grander than the one built by Solomon. Herod also built bridges and cities, and improved the country in many ways; but although he tried to please the people, yet, his being an Edomite, and the quarrels and murders in his own household, made him hated and feared by his Jewish subjects."—*Compiled from Edith Ralph's Bible Stories.*

Judea was now a province of Rome, and Cæsar Augustus was the emperor. "Augustus wished to make a census to enroll all the people of the Roman empire, that he might better divide the vast domain into provinces."—*Butterworth.*

(See "Little Arthur's History of Rome," pages 141, 142, 143; St. Luke, Bible; Ben Hur: Wise Men, Holy Night.)

"Rome rules the European world, and Augustus has but to speak and the nations will hear and obey from the Mediterranean to the Baltic. In this period of concord, an event happened which transcends the glory of Rome, the thoughts of the philosophers, or the music of the poets. There was One who was to preach the brotherhood of man, the rebirth of the soul, the consciousness of God and immortal life, and who was to establish an invisible kingdom in the spirits of men, that should rule all nations and forever endure. The record of this event, as recorded in St. Luke, is one of the most beautiful and transcendent pages of all history.

"The Emperor Augustus, it is said, 'found Rome of brick, and left it in marble.' He found it almost without a literature, and left it heroic with poetry, eloquence, and song, but it is probable that he never so much as heard of this event in the far Syrian province, for he died A. D. 14. Yet His birth in a manger was to topple over all the temples of Rome, and the events of Rome in the future will be dated from it. The works of Augustus have faded and gone, and the birth of the

Christ Child gives them the past days of 1898 years."
—*Butterworth*. Learn song, "Holy Night."

THE BIRTH OF JESUS CHRIST.

ANONYMOUS.

He came not in his people's day
  Of miracle and might,
When awe-struck nations owned their sway,
  And conquest crowned each fight;
When Nature's self with wonder saw
Her ancient power, her boasted law,
  To feeble man give way—
The elements of earth and heaven
Israel stayed—for Judah riven!

Pillar and cloud, Jehovah gave,
  High emblems of his grace;
And clove the rock and smote the wave,
  Moved mountains from their place;
But justice was with mercy blent—
In thunder was the promise sent—
  Fierce lightning veiled his face;
The jealous God, the burning law,
Were all the chosen people saw.

Behold them, pilgrim tribes no more—
  The promised land their own;
And blessings theirs of sea and shore,
  To other realms unknown:
From age to age a favored line
Of mighty kings and seers divine,
  A temple and a throne;
Not then, but in their hour of shame,
Woe, want, and weakness—then he came.

Not in the earthquake's rending force,
  Not in the blasting fire;
Not in the strong wind's rushing course,
  Came He, their soul's desire!

Forerunners of His coming these,
Proclaiming over earth and seas
  As God, His might and ire;
The still, small voice, the hovering dove,
Proved Him Messiah, spoke Him "Love!"

Of life the way, of light the spring
  Eternal, undefiled;
Redeemer, Prophet, Priest, and King—
  Yet came he as a child!
And Zion's favored eye, grown dim,
Knew not her promised Lord in Him,
  The lowly and the mild!
She saw the manger and the tree,
And scornful cried, "Can his be He?"

HEALING THE LEPER.

N. P. WILLIS.

It was noon;
And Helon knelt beside a stagnant pool
In the lone wilderness, and bathed his brow,
Hot with the burning leprosy, and touched
The loathsome water to his fevered lips,
Praying that he might be so blessed—to die!
Footsteps approached, and with no strength to flee,
He drew the covering closer on his lip,
Crying, "Unclean! unclean!" and in the folds
Of the coarse sackcloth shrouding up his face,
He fell upon the earth till they should pass.

Nearer the stranger came, and bending o'er
The leper's prostrate form, pronounced his name—
"Helon!" The voice was like the master-tone
Of a rich instrument—most strangely sweet;
And the dull pulses of disease awoke,
And for a moment beat beneath the hot
And leprous scales with a restoring thrill.
"Helon! arise!" and he forgot his curse,
And rose and stood before him.

                    Love and awe
Mingled in the regard of Helon's eye,
As he beheld the stranger. He was not
In costly raiment clad, nor on his brow
The symbol of a princely lineage wore;
No followers at his back, nor in his hand
Buckler, or sword, or spear; yet in his mien,
Command sat throned serene, and if he smiled,
His eye was blue and calm, as is the sky.
A kingly condescension graced his lips
The lion would have crouched to in his lair.

His garb was simple, and his sandals worn;
His statue modeled with a perfect grace;
His countenance the impress of a god,
Touched with the opening innocence of a child;
His eye was blue and calm, as is the sky
In the serenest noon; his hair unshorn
Fell to his shoulders; and his curling beard
The fullness of perfected manhood bore.

He looked on Helon earnestly awhile,
As if his heart were moved, and stooping down,
He took a little water in his hand
And laid it on his brow, and said, "Be clean."
And lo! the scales fell from him, and his blood
Coursed with delicious coolness through his veins,
And his dry palms grew moist, and on his brow
The dewy softness of an infant stole.
His leprosy was cleansed; and he fell down
Prostrate at Jesus' feet, and worshiped Him.

Extent of the Roman Empire.—The domains over which Augustus held sway stretched from the Atlantic to the Euphrates, and from the Rhine, Danube, and Euxine on the north to the unexplored deserts of Africa and Arabia on the south. The Roman Empire thus included the fairest portions of the known world, surrounding the Mediterranean Sea. More than one hundred millions of people dwelt in these countries, embracing every variety of race, condition, and culture, from the rough barbarian of Gaul to the refined and polished Athenian.

It was by the advice of Augustus that the Romans devoted their energies to the development of the territory already acquired and made few attempts to acquire more. That the same wise policy was continued by those who succeeded him, we may judge from the fact that the empire was limited by nearly the same frontiers from the time of Augustus to that of Constantine.

In the time of Augustus a standing army exceeding one hundred and seventy thousand men guarded the frontiers. "Eight legions were stationed on the Rhine, four on the Danube, three in Spain, two in Dalmatia, eight in Asia and Africa. A body of these troops, known as the *Prætorian Guard*, and comprising nine thousand men, were stationed in Italy as a body-guard to the emperor. A thousand more performed the duties of a city guard in the capital."—*Goodrich*.

"In the succeeding reign this body of soldiers was given a permanent camp alongside the city walls. It soon became a formidable power in the state, and made and unmade emperors at will."—*Myers*.

Revolt of the Germans.—It was the great work of Augustus to establish a frontier on the north as secure and permanent as those in the other directions. In the course of twenty years, the supremacy of Rome was acknowledged in all that part of Germany between the Elbe and the Rhine; but it was not firmly established. "The Germans then consisted of many different nations, all of a warlike character, and not more civilized than the ancient Gauls. They had no towns but lived on their lands which were cultivated by serfs. The country was covered with dense forests, through which were no roads, making it difficult to carry on war there. The Romans had never cared to possess so unattractive a country, but they found it necessary to establish legions on the frontiers and hold the Germans in subjection that they might not make inroads into the empire."—*Goodrich.* In the year 9 A. D., the governor of Germany was Lucius Varus, a brave man and good officer, but wholly incompetent to govern a liberty-loving people like the Germans. When he attempted to introduce the Roman language and laws, a brave chief whom the Romans called Arminius raised a rebellion. "Varus had something of the contempt for the irregular warfare of the Germans that General Braddock had for that of the American Indians." Arminius enticed the Roman Army into the wilds of the Teutoberg Forest and there took a dreadful revenge for the wrongs his people had suffered. The Romans were assaulted by an unseen enemy and completely annihilated. This defeat ended the Roman dominion in Germany, though Germanicus, a Roman general, invaded these regions, six years later, to inflict vengeance for the disaster. (See Myers.)

Great was the dismay when the direful news reached Rome. "The loss of so many of his best soldiers was indeed a sad blow to the emperor, as it was no easy matter, at this period, to raise new legions, for the people in general were unwilling to serve in the armies; so that it had become necessary to emancipate numbers of slaves, and make soldiers of them. The reason of this great dislike for army life was that the soldiers were stationed along the frontiers in fortified camps and were obliged to remain there until they were old men, so that they were completely exiled from their country."—*Goodrich.*

"The aged emperor was broken down by so terrible a reverse at the close of his life, suffered his beard and hair to grow—a mark of mourning—and cried again and again, 'Quintilius Varus, give me back my legions.' He died five years afterwards, asking his friends, in his last moments, whether he had not played his part well in the comedy of life."—*Allen.*

"We now come to the time of the *Ten Cæsars,* whose reigns cover a long epoch of splendor, vice, tragedy, and decay, and embrace some of the darkest pages of human history."—*Butterworth.*

Nero (54 A. D.).—Nero, the last of the emperors at all connected with Augustus, is known as the most wicked of kings. For five years he ruled with justice and clemency, then, putting aside his wise counselors, he entered upon a career filled with crimes which have made his name infamous through all the ages. Among his victims were his mother, his wife, and his stepbrother.

In the tenth year of his reign a conflagration destroyed the greater part of Rome. Nero was suspected of having kindled it in order to enjoy the spectacle. He is reported to have enjoyed a view from a lofty tower, while he chanted the "Sack of Troy" to the music of his lyre. To secure himself, he ascribed the conflagration to the Christians, who, at this time, were a small sect, mostly of the lower classes. The persecution that followed was one of the most cruel recorded in the history of the church. St. Paul and St. Peter, according to tradition, were martyred at this time.

When Rome was destroyed by the Gauls, more than four hundred years before, it was hurriedly built up without system or order (see Invasion of Gauls); now broad avenues were substituted for winding lanes, and handsome stone buildings took the place of unsightly piles of brick or wood.

"Rome arose from her ashes as quickly as Athens after the Persian wars, and the conflagration seemed to have been a blessing in disguise."—*Compiled from Myers and Allen.* (Nero's "Golden House"; see Goodrich and Allen.)

Flavius Vespasian (A. D. 69-79).—The reign of Vespasian was rendered famous by important military achievements abroad and stupendous architectural works at Rome. After one of the most distressing sieges recorded in history, Jerusalem was taken by Titus, son of Vespasian. In the island of Britain the Roman commander, Agricola, subdued or crowded back the native tribes until he had extended the frontiers of the empire into Scotland.

Capture of Jerusalem (A. D. 70).—The independent spirit of the Jews could no longer submit to the tyranny of the Roman officials. They rose in rebellion and Vespasian, during his three years' command in Judea, reduced the whole country into his power, except the capital. When he became emperor his son, Titus, attacked Jerusalem "and reduced it after a siege of over five months, attended by the unutterable horrors of bloodshed, famine, and conflagration. The fanatic party among the Jews confronted the invader with relentless obstinacy. At first they intrenched themselves within the temple, and when this was captured and burned, they withdrew to the heights of Mount Zion, where they continued the defense of the holy city. When this, too, fell, and its buildings were destroyed by fire, Jerusalem had ceased to exist. In the course of time the survivors returned to their old home and built for themselves humble dwellings among its ruins."—*Allen.*

THE DESTRUCTION OF JERUSALEM.
LORD BYRON.

From the last hill that looks on thy once holy dome,
I beheld thee, O Zion, when rendered to Rome;
'Twas the last sun went down, and the flames of thy fall
Flashed back on the last glance I gave to thy wall.

I looked for thy temple, I looked for my home,
And forgot for a moment my bondage to come;
I beheld but the death-fire that fed on thy fane,
And the fast-fettered hands that made vengeance in vain.

On many an eve, the high spot whence I gazed
Had reflected the last beam of day as it blazed;
While I stood on the height and beheld the decline
Of the rays from the mountain that shone on thy shrine.

And now on that mountain I stood on that day,
But I marked not the twilight beam melting away;
Oh! would that the lightning had glared in its stead,
And the thunderbolt burst on the conqueror's head!

But the gods of the Pagan shall never profane
The shrine where Jehovah disdained not to reign;
And scattered and scorned as Thy people may be,
Our worship, O Father! is only for Thee.

"On his return to Rome, Titus celebrated a triumph for his hard-won victory; and a few years later a triumphal arch was built upon the highest spot in the Sacred Way, on the walls of which was carved—still to be seen—a representation of that sacred candlestick of the Jewish temple which had been carried among the trophies of his triumph.

"The greatest architectural work of this reign was the Flavian Amphitheater, better known as the Colosseum, to this day the most magnificent of the remains of ancient Rome."—*Allen*.

(See page 205, "Little Arthur's History of Rome.")

Reign of Titus.—"In his short reign of two years Titus won the title, the "Delight of Mankind." He had his father's military gifts, with a milder and more kindly disposition." Having let a day pass by without some act of kindness performed he is said to have exclaimed reproachfully, "I have lost a day."

The only event of importance in the reign of Titus was the greatest eruption of Vesuvius that has ever been known, causing the destruction of the cities of Herculaneum and Pompeii. "The cities were buried beneath showers of cinders, ashes, and streams of volcanic sand. Pliny the Elder, the great naturalist, venturing too near the mountain to investigate the phenomenon, lost his life."—*Myers*. "His nephew, Pliny the Younger, has given a most interesting account of this event in one of his letters." (See Goodrich's "History of Rome"; "Lit-tle Arthur's History" Supplementary Readers; "Last Days of Pompeii," by Bulwer.)

The Five Good Emperors.—After the death of the

last of the Cæsars, the senate claimed the right of electing the rulers. Nerva, Trajan, Hadrian, Antoninus Pius, and Marcus Aurelius, by their wise administrations, brought the government to a humane and equitable standing. The morals of the people steadily improved and there was less vice at this period than one hundred or two hundred years before.

"*Marcus Aurelius*, the last of the five good emperors, was the noblest of all the characters of later Roman history. When a mere child he preferred study to the splendors of the court. At the age of twelve he took the philosophic mantle as an indication of his chosen pursuits. He accepted the principles of the Stoics, adopted their habits, and found his delight in denying himself for the sake of the good of his soul. (See page 115 and 116, "Little Arthur's History of Rome.") Though heir to the grandest throne in the world, he overcame pride, and maintained simple habits, and in an age of fiery passions he acquired a serene disposition and became an example of beauty as well as simplicity of character. His judgment became so clear that Antoninus Pius, his father-in-law, associated him in the government many years before he died."—*Butterworth.*

" It was a hard fate which associated this upright and conscientious prince with the most disturbed and calamitous events of the century, and made his reign a critical moment in the downfall of the empire."—*Allen.* After the long period of quiet and prosperity under Hadrian and Antoninus Pius the empire was suddenly invaded by swarms of Northern barbarians. "Aurelius was a man of peace, but he was obliged to carry on defensive wars, and led his army in person, enduring the lot of a common soldier.

"He was so much of a Stoic as to be blind to Christianity, and opposed to it, although he has surpassed most Christian kings in living the principles of the Christian faith. He seems to have thought Christianity to be an immoral superstition, as it was then called, and if it be good that his philosophy yet transcended it. In one of his campaigns against the German tribes on the Danube, he was shut up in a barren defile where there was no water, and his army seemed about to perish with thirst, when a Christian legion in his army knelt down and prayed. A cloud arose followed by a deluge of rain. The Christians attributed the rain to their faith, but Aurelius to Jupiter. The scene is represented in art in a very dramatic way, the soldiers catching the water as it fell on their shields. The Christian soldiers who thus called on God became known as the Thundering Legion.

"The reign of Aurelius was troubled by plague, earthquake and famine, but amid it all, like a Roman Job, he held that all things that happened were for the good of all, and that the Divine wisdom was to be praised in the darkest events of life. His strength of character grew with years, and he sacrificed self for the good of others until Rome looked upon him as a divinity." He died at Vienna in the prime of life while still engaged in protecting his country from invasion.

"At his death the empire went into sincere mourning. The senate voted him a god, Rome set up his images for veneration and the world has never ceased to hold his character in high esteem.

"But it is by his published works, written in Greek, that he now lives in influence. Except in the teachings of the gospel, perhaps no man ever saw truth in a clearer light, or wrote more sublime precepts for the guidance of mankind. Extracts from the 'Meditations,' of Marcus Aurelius:

"I. 'The whole world is one commonwealth.'

"II. 'That which is not for the interest of the whole is not for the interest of one.'

"III. 'Cease your complaint and you are not injured.'

"IV. 'No man can injure thee unless he makes thy character worse.'

"V. 'A thing is neither better or worse for being praised. No virtues stand in need of any good word, or are worse for a bad one. An emerald will shine, though the world be silent.'

"VI. 'Be always doing something serviceable to mankind.'"—*Butterworth*.

(See "Little Arthur's History.")

New Causes of the Decline of the Empire.—We have already noted in the Decay of the Republic the principal sources of decline; such as the degradation of free industry by slave labor. In the reign of Aurelius new causes of decline seemed to be added. A destructive inundation of the Tiber was followed by distress and famine. A few years after this the eastern army brought the plague with it from Asia and the infection was communicated to every province through which the legions passed. The violence of the pestilence did not abate for several years.

To the panic of the plague was added the terror of the barbarian invasion. With diminishing population and diminishing resources, the devoted Aurelius checked the inroads of the barbarians but he could not subdue them. —*Adapted from Allen.*

Persecution of the Christians.—The people thought that these repeated calamities—war, inundation, famine, pestilence, barbarian inroads—must have been sent by the gods as a punishment for some national guilt. As the Christians deserted the temples and refused to worship the gods under whose protection the state had prospered, they were accused of angering the gods. Accustomed as they were to holding their meetings at night, and often in secret, they were looked upon as enemies of the state and persecuted even by the best rulers, Trajan, Marcus Aurelius, and Diocletian.—*Adapted from Allen and Myers.*

The rising faith, however, was only strengthened by opposition. The heroism of the martyrs extorted the admiration of their enemies and won multitudes to the persecuted faith. Polycarp, Bishop of Smyrna, exclaimed, when brought before the tribunal and urged to curse Christ, 'Eighty-six years have I served Him, and He has done me nothing but good; how could I curse Him, my Lord and Savior!" As the flames rose around him he thanked God that he was deemed worthy of such a death. In the times of dread and distress which accompanied the downfall of the empire, the Gospel alone brought the consolation that satisfied men's souls. The triumph of Christianity was near at hand.

Decline of the Empire (180 to 284 A. D.).—Assailed by vice, corruption, and disease within and fierce barbarians without, the empire no longer recovered from the attacks. The army became the governing power and the emperor its servant. The Prætorian guard put up the imperial power at auction and sold it to the highest bidder. The people had become so debased that they were willing to close their eyes to the vices of the emperors, and even to participate therein. They were content if they were fed daily from the public granaries and amused by the cruel sports of the arena. "The emperor Valerian was taken prisoner by the Persian king, who carried him about in chains and used him as a footstool in mounting his horse." After nearly a century of disorder and misrule, the barbarians had passed the frontiers and were occupying the provinces. The empire seemed on the point of falling when it was restored for a time by five energetic rulers, who succeeded each other.—*Adapted.*

Reforms of Diocle'tian (A. D. 284).—A new method of government was introduced by Diocletian. He observed that the empire was too large and too varied in nationality to be successfully governed by one emperor. The empire was therefore divided so it could be ruled from two centers: Milan became the western capital and Nicomedia the eastern. Each emperor received the title of Augustus and associated with himself a general or Cæsar, who succeed him to the throne. The government now became absolute, all authority and law emanating from the emperor. An oriental monarchy had taken the place of the Empire of the Cæsars. By the wise administration of Diocle'tian new vigor was awakened in all parts of the empire. "War waged at once in Persia, Egypt, Britain, and Germany, but the Roman eagles conquered every foe."

"After the joint reign of Diocle'tian and Maxim'ian had for about nineteen years restored the glory of Rome, they of their own accord gave up the purple, leaving the imperial power to the two Cæsars. Diocle'tian contentedly passed the evening of his life in rural occupations. To Maximian, who tried to induce him to reassume the scepter, the old monarch wrote, 'Could you but see the cabbages I raise, you would no longer talk to me of empire!'"—*Quackenbos.*

The Catacombs.—The growth of the city of Rome led to the formation of immense quarries under the streets, suburbs, and immediate neighborhood. The stone taken from these quarries was used for building purposes and the caverns grew with the demand for material. These caverns or subterranean rooms and galleries were called catacombs. They became the hiding-place of persecuted people, outlaws, and criminals."
—*Butterworth.* In the second and third centuries the Christians sought refuge in the catacombs. "Here they buried their dead, and on the walls of the chambers sketched rude symbols of their confident faith. It was in the darkness of these subterranean abodes that Christian art had its beginnings."—*Myers.* The last and severest of the persecutions of the church took place in the reign of Diocletian.

Constantine the Great.—The succession planned by Diocletian was disregarded after his successor died. Constantine, the Cæsar in Britain, was made sole emperor by his troops. But it was not until after eighteen years had passed that he succeeded in overthrowing his many rivals and became the supreme ruler (324 A. D.).

During the campaign against one of these he is said to have been miraculously converted to Christianity. According to the legend the scene of the event was near Rome, which city Constantine was approaching to engage in battle with the rival emperor, Maxentius. It was the afternoon of the 27th of October. Constantine was invoking the gods for the success of his cause. Suddenly there appeared a pillar of light in the sky in the form of a cross, and beneath it the inscription: "*In hoc signo vinces,*" "In this sign thou shalt conquer."

The standard adopted was made thus :-

"A long spear plated with gold, with a transverse piece at the top in the form of a cross, to which was fastened a four-square purple banner embroidered with gold and beset with precious stones. Above the cross was a crown overlaid with gold and gems, within which was placed the sacred symbol, the first two letters of the name of Christ in Greek.

"Under this banner Constantine, having overcome Maxentius, entered Rome in triumph, and was hailed by the Christian population with great rejoicing.

"Thus the waning autumn of 312 witnessed the beginning of the end of the heathen rites of more than a thousand years, and the advent of the faith that has come to possess the civilized world. We may credit or not the vision of the cross, the event of the downfall of ancient gods and the acceptance of the gospel of Christ is certain. The ancient Rome vanished, a new Rome came.

"The master of the Roman World, having become a Christian, aspired to found a city which should be dedicated to the enlightened faith from the beginning." Rome was hallowed by the divine presence and sacred associations of the heathen deities. Many of the inhabitants, still devoted to the ancient faith, strongly opposed this abandonment of the old national deities. (See speech of Camillus, by Livy.) Rome had for a long time been too far remote from the center of population, wealth, and culture to be the capital of this wide extended empire. After long and careful deliberation, Byzantium was chosen by Constantine as the site for a new Rome that should be a worthy rival of the old. His wisdom in the selection of this commanding situation has been universally recognized. Byzantium occupied the triangular space between the Golden Horn, an inlet of the Bosporus, and the Propontis. The walls of the new city were laid out at a distance of two miles outside of those of the old. The presence of the court and the commercial advantages of the situation contributed to the building up of the city when the empire did not flourish. Enormous sums were spent in embellishing the new metropolis with a capitol, amphitheater, splendid palaces, and churches, the chief of which was the St. Sophia. This new capital, called Constantinople, from its founder, was to defy the barbarians and endure a thousand years after Rome had fallen.

"After Constantine had fixed his residence in the new

capital, he adopted oriental manners. He affected the gorgeous attire of the Persian monarchs, and wore a diadem covered with pearls and gems. He substituted flowing robes of silk embroidered with flowers, for the austere garb of Rome, or the unadorned purple of the first emperors. He filled his palaces with spies and parasites, and lavished the wealth of the empire upon stately architecture."—*Goodrich and Butterworth.*

The First General Council of the Church.—"By a decree issued from Milan, A. D. 313, Christianity was made the state religion, and in A. D. 325 a General Council of the church was held at Nicæa, in Asia Minor. The doctrine of Arius, who denied the divinity of Christ, was denounced, and a formula of Christian faith adopted, which is known as the Nicene Creed."—*Myers.*

ROMAN CONQUEST OF GREAT BRITAIN.

Physical Features.—(See geography.)

Earliest Glimpses of British History.—Several hundred years before the Christian era it is supposed that the Phœnicians visited England. Their chief object was to obtain tin, which was procured from the mines of Cornwall. Hence the Casterides, or Tin Isles, was the ancient designation of the British Isles.

Britons.—"The original inhabitants of England, Ireland, and Scotland seem to have been of the same Celtic stock which first peopled France and Spain, though they were divided into numerous tribes." These people were called Britons, and their country was known as Britain. "A few among the more southern tribes practiced agriculture in a rude way, and wore artificial cloths for dress. They had also war-chariots in great numbers."— *Goodrich*. "These chariots were not quite breast high in front and open at the back, contained one man to drive and two or three others to fight, all standing up. The horses which drew them were so well trained, that they would tear at full gallop, over the most stony ways, and even through the woods, dashing down their master's enemies beneath their hoofs, and cutting them to pieces with the blades of swords, or scythes, which were fastened to the wheels and stretched out beyond the car on each side, for that cruel purpose. In a moment while at full speed, the horses would stop at the driver's command. The men within would leap out, deal blows about them with their swords like hail, leap on the horses or spring back into the chariots, and, as soon as they were safe, the horses tore away again."—*Dickens*.

"The women, like those of the American Indian, were practiced in basket-making, the material being the twigs of willows. They also sewed together the skins of animals for dress, their thread being made of leather or vegetable fibers, and their needles of pieces of bone."— *Goodrich*.

Condition of Country.—"The whole country was covered with forests and swamps. The greater part of it was very misty and cold. There were no roads, no bridges, no streets, no houses, that you would think deserving of the name. A town was nothing but a collection of straw-covered huts hidden in a thick wood, with a ditch all around and a low wall, made of mud, or the trunks of trees placed one upon another."—*Dickens*.

"Such was the condition of the country and people when Julius Cæsar, having completed the subjugation of Gaul, began to think of adding the island of Britain to his conquests. The white chalk cliffs of Dover, from which Britain had also the name of Albion, could be seen from the coast of Gaul, and as Cæsar's ambition knew no bounds, he doubtless thought that this strange country invited him to its conquest.

Cæsar's Invasion.—"Having decided to undertake an expedition against it, he assembled the merchants who had traded with the Britons for hides and tin, and made inquiries respecting the manners, customs, and power of the people of Britain. We may suppose that Cæsar had little dread of meeting such a savage people as the Britons with his well-disciplined troops. He probably learned, too, that the people were divided into many small tribes, governed by independent rulers, who did not agree very well among themselves.

"He embarked his troops at Calais, and in a few hours reached the coast of Britain near Dover. The Britons had heard of his coming, and were assembled to prevent his landing. Their painted bodies gave them a most terrific appearance, and their savage yells made even the Romans hesitate to attack them.

"At last a standard-bearer jumped into the sea, and advanced with the eagle, which was the Roman standard, towards the enemy, crying aloud, 'Follow me, soldiers, unless you will betray the Roman eagle into the hands of the enemy. I, at least, will discharge my duty to Cæsar and to my country.' Animated by this speech, and excited by his example, the soldiers plunged into the sea, and waded to the land, in spite of all the Britons could do. Cæsar remained about three weeks on the island, during which he gained many battles. He then granted a peace to the Britons, upon condition that they should pay tribute to the Romans.

Second Invasion (54 B. C.).—"The Britons neglected to perform their engagements, and in the year 54 B. C. Cæsar again invaded the island. Landing, as before, at Deal, he advanced into the country. The Britons had now united their forces under one chief named Cassivelaunus. Still they were defeated in every battle. Having brought the people to submission, and compelled them to give him many of their chief men as hostages, Cæsar returned to Rome. As no troops were left in Britain to maintain the authority of Rome, the Britons soon threw off all marks of subjection, and the tribute remained unpaid. The civil dissensions among the Romans themselves long prevented their taking any measures to compel the payment.

Civilization.—"An intercourse was, however, kept up with Rome. Many of the chief persons of Britain visited that city, and some of the young men were educated there. By this means the Britons began to improve in their manners and habits. The mantle of skins was replaced by one of cloth, and close trousers were introduced. They likewise adopted a vest, a tunic, fitting tight to the body and reaching just below the waist. Their shoes were still made of the skins of some animal with their hair outwards.

"They soon began to coin money. When metals were

first introduced as money, their value was determined by weight. The seller having agreed to accept a certain quantity of gold or silver for his goods, the buyer cut off that quantity from the piece of that metal in his possession, and, having weighed it, delivered it to the seller, and received the goods.

"The invasion of the Romans had made the Britons acquainted with the use of tools; and stout galleys took the place of frail boats made of osiers and the flexible branches of trees, covered with skins of oxen, in which they had hitherto navigated the stormy seas around their islands.

Third Invasion.—"At length, in the year 43 A. D., being 97 years from the first invasion by Cæsar, the Romans determined to make another attempt to conquer Britain. An army of 50,000 men was collected and sent into the island, under the command of Aulus Plautius. The Britons fought bravely for their liberty, but could not withstand the Roman discipline. Their principal chief, named Caractacus, and his family, were taken prisoners. They were all sent to Rome, and the king and his wife and two daughters were made to walk through the streets loaded with chains. Observing the splendor of the great city he could not forbear exclaiming, 'Alas! how is it possible that people possessed of such magnificence at home should envy me my humble cottage in Britain.'"

"Notwithstanding their victories, the Romans made little progress in the conquest of the island. Suetonius Paulinus, one of their most skillful generals, resolved to adopt a new method. He observed that the Druids were the most inveterate enemies of the Romans, and that it was their influence which kept up the spirit of the people.

Druids.—"The Druids were the priests and law-givers of the Britons. The chiefs commanded the forces in time of war, but all other power was in the hands of the Druids. The laws of the Britons were composed in verse, and the only record of them was in the memory of the Druids. The old taught them to the young, and thus the knowledge of them was kept up from one generation to another.

". So great was the veneration in which they were held that, when two hostile armies, with daggers drawn and spears extended, were about to engage in battle, the request of the Druids was sufficient to calm their rage, and to induce them to shield their daggers, and separate in peace.

"The Druids believed that it was displeasing to the Deity to worship within walls, or under roofs. They worshiped, therefore, in the open air in groves of particular trees. The favorite was the strong and spreading oak, and in all their ceremonies they were crowned with garlands of its leaves. In the center of the grove was the rude altar of stones upon which sacrifices were offered. The victims were not sheep and oxen alone, but the prisoners taken in war were considered as a most acceptable offering.

" The principal residence of the Druids was in the little island of Anglesea. Suetonius resolved to make himself master of this stronghold. The Britons endeavored to prevent the landing of their troops. The women and priests mingled with the soldiers on the shore, and running about with burning torches in their hands and tossing their long hair, they terrified the astonished Romans more by their shrieks and howlings, than by the appearance of the armed forces. But the Romans soon recovered their spirits, and, marching boldly forward, speedily put an end to all resistance. Meanwhile the Britons took advantage of the absence of Suetonius. Headed by Boadicea, a brave queen, they attacked and destroyed the Roman settlements. There were many of these which were quite flourishing. London, which at the first invasion was a forest, had now become a rich and populous city.

Boadicea Defeated.—"Suetonius was obliged to abandon this place to the fury of the Britons. It was entirely destroyed, and more than 70,000 Romans and other strangers were put to death. But he soon had a most cruel revenge; with his little army of 10,000 men, he attacked the Britons and left 80,000 of them dead upon the field of battle. Boadicea, in despair at this defeat, poisoned herself. (See poem.)

Agricola in Britain.—"The Romans now easily established themselves all over Britain, and built towns and castles, and were entire masters of the country. Julius Agricola, one of their generals, was a very good, as well as a brave man. He endeavored to reconcile the Britons to the Roman government by introducing their arts and sciences. He encouraged them to engage in agriculture, which the Romans considered the most honorable employment. He also persuaded them to learn the Latin language. He succeeded so well in his endeavors that the Britons soon began to esteem it a privilege to be a part of the Roman empire. Indeed, they derived other advantages besides the increase of comfort which a knowledge of the Roman arts had brought them. The northern part of the island, called Caledonia, and now Scotland, was inhabited by the Scots and Picts, a wild and warlike people, who made incursions into the country of Britain, and, after destroying everything that came in their way, retired into their bleak and barren mountains.

Whenever they ventured to stand a battle in the open field they were defeated by the Romans; but they seldom did this. They generally retired as the Roman troops advanced. As soon as the latter were withdrawn from their neighborhood they again commenced their depredations. Agricola caused a line of forts to be built across Scotland, thus shutting out the marauders. The country now remained at peace for many years, during which the Romans occupied themselves in making roads, many of which are still remaining, and in building strong and massive castles, the ruins of which are still to be seen.

Wall between Scotland and England.—"But the forts did not prove a sufficient defense against the Picts and Scots, who renewed their incursions upon the more cultivated parts of the island. The Emperor Hadrian, who visited Britain, caused a rampart of earth to be erected. This, however, proved too weak, and in the year 207 A. D. the Emperor Severus came to Britain with a determination to conquer Caledonia. The nature of the country and the bravery of the people prevented his succeeding; so he contented himself with building an immense stone wall, twelve feet high and eight feet thick, quite across the country, from the river Tyne to Solway Firth, many parts of which are still to be seen.

Introduction of Christianity.—"For a long time everything went on so quietly that little mention is made of the affairs of this island by any historian. The people were governed by Roman officers, and Christianity was introduced, making considerable progress, it is believed, before the end of the first century. About the year 448, the Romans were compelled to withdraw their troops from the distant provinces, and, among the rest, from Britain, to defend their city against the barbarous tribes of the north of Europe.

The Romans Abandon Britain.—"Before the Romans left the island, they repaired the wall built by Severus. But as walls are of very little use without brave and well-armed men to defend them, the Roman general instructed the Britons in the art of making and of using the several kinds of weapons. He then departed with his troops, telling the people that, as they would never again have assistance from the Romans, they had better learn to take care of themselves. Thus the Romans departed from the island, after having had possession of it nearly five hundred years, if we reckon from the first invasion of Julius Cæsar."—*Goodrich*.

BOADICEA.
COWPER.

When the British warrior queen,
  Bleeding from the Roman rods,
Sought, with an indignant mien,
  Counsel of her country's gods,

Sage beneath the spreading oak,
    Sat the Druid, hoary chief;
Every burning word he spoke
    Full of rage and full of grief.

"Princess! if our aged eyes
    Weep upon thy matchless wrongs,
'Tis because resentment ties
    All the terrors of our tongues.

"Rome shall perish—write that word
    In the blood that she has spilt;
Perish, hopeless and abhorr'd,
    Deep in ruin as in guilt.

"Rome, for empire far renown'd,
    Tramples on a thousand states;
Soon her pride shall kiss the ground—
    Hark! the Gaul is at her gates!

"Other Romans shall arise,
    Heedless of a soldier's name,
Sounds, not arms, shalt win the prize,
    Harmony the path to fame.

"Then the progeny that springs
    From the forests of our land,
Arm'd with thunder, clad with wings,
    Shall a wider world command.

"Regions Cæsar never knew
    Thy posterity shall sway;
Where his eagles never flew,
    None invincible as they."

Such the bard's prophetic words,
    Pregnant with celestial fire,
Bending as he swept the chords
    Of his sweet but awful lyre.

She, with all a monarch's pride,
    Felt them in her bosom glow;
Rush'd to battle, fought, and died;
    Dying hurl'd them at the foe.

"Ruffians, pitiless as proud,
 Heaven awards the vengeance due;
 Empire is on us bestow'd,
 Shame and ruin wait for you."

FALL OF ROME.

Barbarian Invasions (Character of Germans) (See Emerton's History).—"In the latter part of the fourth century a host of savage Huns burst into Europe. The Huns were a people, surely not of German stock, nor even of the Aryan race. They came from the north of Asia, beyond the great wall of China, passed through the 'gateway of nations,' between the Caspian Sea and the Ural Mountains, and fell upon the distant settlements of the East-Goths in the valley of the Don. (Story of Goths. See page 25, Emerton's "Introduction to Study of Middle Ages.")

"The Huns were frightful little men, living almost wholly on horseback, sweeping over the country like a whirlwind and leaving only destruction behind them. They had the olive skins of the Orientals, their hair was worn long and tied into a knot behind. Their noses were so much turned up that the frightened Romans fancied that they had nothing but two holes in the middle of their faces. They seemed hardly to deserve the name of human beings; nothing could resist them. The East-Goths surrendered and were forced to join the Huns in in their attack upon the West-Goths.

Visigoths.—"These latter, in their despair, begged the Roman Emperor Valens to give them shelter, and were allowed to come over and settle in Mœsia, south of the

Danube. It was understood that the Romans should furnish them with weapons and supplies, for which they should pay by defending the river against any new attack. The West-Goths seem to have kept their part of the agreement, but the Roman officers were careless in their treatment of the barbarians. One trouble led to another, until finally the Germans broke out into open revolt. The *Emperor Valens*, without waiting for any help from the West, gave battle near Adrianople, in Thrace, and was utterly defeated. He himself was killed in the retreat, and the Visigoths found themselves suddenly within the empire, with no army to oppose them, and, as it seemed, the promise of endless plunder.

"The battle of *Adrianople* was one of the decisive battles of the world. It taught the Germans that they could beat the legions in open fight, and that henceforth it was for them to name the price of peace. It broke once for all the Rhine-Danube frontier. Swarms of fighting men, Ostrogoths as well as Visigoths, came pouring into the empire. At the death of Valens, who had been ruler of the East, his nephew Gratian was left as ruler of the West. He had sense enough to see that he could not hope to govern the whole of the great Roman empire, and called upon *Theodosius*, a Spaniard, and a man of well-proven ability, to take the government of the East. He saw that it was hopeless to think of driving out the Germans, and that the best way to manage them was to keep them quarreling with each other. He made treaties by which the Visigoths were given lands in Thrace, and the Ostrogoths in Pannonia, between the Mur and the Danube. They were to receive regular pay in money and were to defend the frontier. Their vanity was tickled with the fine-sounding name of 'allies,' and their leaders were placed in the highest positions in the state. The confidential minister of Theodosius was a German, a Vandal named *Stilicho*, son of a chieftain who had served with his 'chestnut-haired squadrons,' in the armies of Valens. But the Gothic warriors were not long to be bound with paper chains. There were always some among them who despised the service of Rome, and longed to be masters instead of servants. This restless ambition for conquest brought forward the greatest leader of the Visigothic name, the famous *Alaric*. With him for their leader the nation took up its march once more, with the fixed purpose of finding lands in the very heart of the empire, where they might settle once for all. Their taste of Roman ways seems only to have made them want more, and they were already losing something of the wildness they had brought from their Northern home. The great Theodosius died just as Alaric was chosen leader of the Visigoths. His empire was divided between his sons, *Arcadius*, in the East, and *Honorius*, in the West, and was never to be united again. The sons were a wretched pair. With ruin staring him in the face, Honorius shut himself up in Ravenna amidst the marshes of the Po, and left the defense of the empire to Stilicho.

"Alaric at first fixed his attention upon Greece, and moved his army southward into the center of the Peloponnesus. Arcadius, the Eastern emperor, had no force strong enough to resist the assault, and Greece was only saved by a brilliant exploit of Stilicho, who crossed the

Adriatic Sea and shut Alaric up within the province of Arcadia. He dared not risk a battle, however, and was glad to purchase the retreat of Alaric by a renewed commission as defender of Illyria. Nothing could have been better for Alaric. He gave up Greece only to be quartered in a rich and defenseless province close upon the borders of Italy. Every step of the Visigothic conquerors shows them to be emerging more and more from the condition of mere fighters, and becoming, in a truer sense of the word, a nation.

"Their new quarters sufficed for them only about three years. Again the nation in arms moved forward into the rich valley of the Po. The empire was now fully alarmed. From all the most distant frontiers the legions were summoned in hot haste to Rome, and formed by Stilicho into a great army, with which he waited for Alaric near Pollentia, on the river Tanarus. A terrific battle was fought here, in which Alaric was, if not badly beaten, at least turned back in his career. He was driven out of Italy, and sought shelter in Pannonia. The government actually believed that the barbarians were disposed of forever. It had no conception of the masses of men waiting their opportunity to pour through the breach of the defenseless frontier. Honorius kept on amusing himself at Ravenna. Until now he had shown for Stilicho the respect and confidence due to the savior of Rome. Stilicho had married the niece and adopted daughter of Theodosius, and had given his own two daughters successively in marriage to Honorious. It seemed as if his fortunes were bound up with the very life of the imperial family. But now, at the very moment when the only man who could hold a Roman army against the barbarians was more needed than ever, the mad folly, which was destroying the empire more surely than her outward enemies, drove Honorious to cause the murder of his faithful servant. Some jealous rival had made him believe that so much power was dangerous to his tottering throne.

"Alaric, away up in Illyria, knew better how to value the only man who had ever defeated him. The death of Stilicho was a signal for a new invasion. The Gothic leader, Christian though he was, believed himself to be in the hands of Destiny. A voice, it was said, had come to him out of the sacred grove, saying, 'You will reach the city,' and he knew that the 'city' could be none other than Rome. The Goths, strengthened by their six years of rest, swept rapidly southward past Ravenna, where Honorius still kept his useless self, marched straight to Rome and began a regular siege. It was the first time for eight hundred years that Rome had seen a foreign enemy before her walls. The citizens could not yet believe that the holy city was in danger. Not until hunger and pestilence began to do their awful work did they send to ask terms of Alaric.

"'Give me all your gold, all your silver, all your movables and all your barbarian slaves, or the siege goes on.' 'What, then, will you leave us?' 'Your lives.'

"But perhaps Alaric was only in a sort of grim humor, making fun of the half-starved ambassadors. He finally agreed to accept a fixed sum in gold, silver, silken tunics, scarlet hides, and pepper, together with ample lands in the north of Italy. The mad young emperor at Ravenna, putting on a show of courage when it was too late, refused to agree to these terms. Alaric promptly renewed the siege, but this time in quite a different fashion. It is as if a strange awe at the name of Rome held him back from actual violence. He was in constant negotiation with the citizens, and even went so far as to set up and maintain, for a few months, a rival emperor. He now proposed still more moderate terms, which Honorius again refused. And the third assault on Rome began. A vigorous attack made a breach in the walls, and the city was in the hands of the enemy. It is curious to see, how, in the course of his long negotiation with the Romans, Alaric had come to be half a Roman himself. He was no longer a mere barbarian chieftain, eager only for a fight and careless of the future. He was the conqueror of Rome, and felt himself somehow to be thus a part of the wonderful civilization he saw about him. He commanded his followers to respect the churches and their property. We have no reason to believe that the buildings of the city suffered very greatly. What the Germans wanted was movable plunder, and laden with this, they set out for the south of Italy. Rome, after all these months of famine and pestilence, was anything but an agreeable residence.

"Besides, the Germans had not yet learned to live in cities. Their object, as shown by the frequent treaties, was to secure a permanent home, when they should find a country suited to their mind. The later historian of their race says that Alaric meant to conquer Sicily and sail over to Africa. Certainly he gathered ships at Rhegium, and is said to have been prevented only by a storm from crossing to Messina.

"Before he could renew his preparations he died suddenly, the first great barbarian victim to the deadly climate of Italy, which was to be her best defense against the Northern invader. The Visigoths forced their Roman captives to turn the channel of the river Busentum, dug their leader's grave in the dry bed of the stream, let the waters flow back and murdered all who had done the work, that the burial place of Alaric might ever remain a mystery.

"The capture of Rome made a deep impression upon the men of that day. They had been so accustomed to think of it as a sacred place, that the fall of the city seemed to them like the end of the world.

"How much the Emperor Honorius cared for Rome we may judge from a story, which, whether true or not, shows what was thought of him at that time. An officer rushed into his presence, and told him that Rome had perished. 'What!' cried the Emperor, 'she was feeding from my hand an hour ago.' He was much relieved when told that it was not his favorite hen 'Roma,' but only the capital of his empire that had perished.

"Alaric is to be remembered as the man who pointed out the way which so many others of his race were to follow. He was a great military genius, whose equal was not found among the many leaders who built upon his plans. We may believe that upon this last expedition the great bulk of the property of the Visigoths had been left behind with the women and children somewhere in the Alpine country, and it may have been this which led them now to give up the African plan, and under the lead of Adolf, brother-in-law of Alaric, to march out of Italy as they had come in.

"More and more, the distinction between Roman and barbarian disappears. The sister of Honorius, the beautiful and learned Placidia, taken captive in Rome, marries the Gothic leader. Adolf brings the Visigoths back into the service of the empire. They pass over into Gaul, and thence across the Pyrenees into Spain. Already parts of various German tribes had taken the same road, and were helping themselves to the lands of the empire on both sides of the mountains. Under Wallia, the successor of Adolf, the Visigoths, serving as the allies of Rome, subdued the rival invaders, and brought back the country for a time to the Roman allegiance.

The Kingdom of Visigoths.—"The price of this service was a new and final grant of land in Spain and the South of Gaul, extending from the river Loire beyond the Pyrenees and over the greater part of the peninsula. Here the wanderings of the Visigoths came to an end. They made use of what they had learned from Rome to found a great and prosperous kingdom, with Toulouse as its capital. It was to last entire until the beginning of the sixth century, when the growth of the all-conquering Franks on the northern border reduced its Gallic portion to a Frankish province. The Spanish portion kept up an independent life, until, in the early part of the eighth century, the storm of the Mohammedan invasion from the south swept it out of existence."—*Emerton*.

(Stories of Vandals, Huns, and Burgundians. See Emerton's History, "Introduction to Middle Ages.")

Sack of Rome by the Vandals.—The Vandals, another German tribe from the Baltic, had found their way across the Strait of Gibraltar into Africa. Gen'seric, their leader, founded an empire at Carthage, and they became a race of bold, successful pirates. They were a common terror to all the nations on the Mediterranean, plundering and destroying everywhere they went. Since their day, wanton destruction of property has been called "Vandalism." In 455 Gen'seric's ships cast anchor in the Tiber "and came swooping down upon the city of Rome from the port of Ostia, expecting to be met by an army of Roman youth. Instead of this there issued from the gates a procession of venerable clergy, led by Bishop Leo. The barbarian conqueror promised to spare the unresisting people, but for fourteen days the city was given over to pillage, and all that remained of Roman wealth, of public or private treasure, the gems of maid and matron, the holy decorations of the temples and altars, the crown, the purple, and the insignia of state, all were transported to the vessels of Gen'seric.

"So Rome, that had robbed the world, was robbed by the world in the weakness begotten by the spoils of nations. The measure that she had meted was meted out to her again." The Roman spirit had decayed in the years of riches, triumph, and so-called glory. In the year 490, the last phantom monarch of Rome, Romulus Augustulus, laid down his useless scepter at the command of Odoacer, the barbarian, who was now king of the land of Æneas, of Romulus, Tullius, Cincinnatus, Regulus, and Aurelius.

"Prosperity had proved fatal to Roman virtue, and the loss of character was a loss of spirit, and honor, and valor. The hardy giants of the northern lands held her at their mercy, and the Queen of Empires, after all her triumphs, grovelled now at the barbarians' chariot wheels."—*Butterworth.*

ROME.

LORD BYRON.

The Niobe of nations! there she stands,
   Childless and crownless, in her voiceless woe,
An empty urn within her withered hands,
   Whose holy dust was scattered long ago:
The Scipios' tomb contains no ashes now,
   The very sepulchers lie tenantless
Of their heroic dwellers: dost thou flow,
   O Tiber, through a marble wilderness?
   Rise, with thy yellow waves, and mantle her distress.

The Goth, the Christian, Time, War, Flood, and Fire,
   Have dealt upon the seven-hilled city's pride;
She saw her glories star by star expire,
And up the steep barbarian monarchs ride,
Where the car climbed the Capitol; far and wide
   Temple and tower went down, nor left a site:—
Chaos of ruins! who shall trace the void,
   O'er the dim fragments cast a lunar light,
   And say, "here was, or is," where all is doubly night?

The double night of ages, and of her,
   Night's daughter, Ignorance, hath wrapt and wrap
All round us; we but feel our way to err:
   The ocean hath his chart, the stars their map,

And Knowledge spreads them on her ample lap;
But Rome is as the desert, where we steer
Stumbling o'er recollections; now we clap
   Our hands, and cry "Eureka!" it is clear—
When but some false mirage of ruin rises near.

Alas! the lofty city! and alas!
   The trebly hundred triumphs! and the day
When Brutus made the dagger's edge surpass
   The conqueror's sword, in bearing Fame away!
Alas, for Tully's voice and Virgil's lay,
   And Livy's pictured page!—but these shall be
Her resurrection; all beside—decay,
   Alas for Earth, for never shall we see
That brightness in her eye she bore when Rome was free!

LIST OF WORKS

Which, by kind permission of the publishers or authors (where copyright is in force), are quoted from or referred to in this work.

LEW WALLACE's "Ben Hur," published by Harper & Brothers.
P. U. N. MYERS' "Eastern Countries and Greece" and "Ancient History," published by Ginn & Co.
CHARLOTTE YONGE's "Young Folks' History of Greece," by Estes and Lauriat.
S. G. GOODRICH's "English History," by E. H. Butler & Co.
W. C. BRYANT's poems of "The Ages" and "Forest Hymn," by D. Appleton & Co.
ALLEN's "Short History of the Roman People," by Ginn & Co.
BUTTERWORTH's "Little Arthur's History of Rome," by Thomas Y. Crowell & Co.
EMERTON's "Introduction to Middle Ages," by Ginn & Co.
DR. GOLDSMITH's "History of Greece," by Thomas Cowperthwait & Co. 1841.
QUACKENBOS' "School History of the World," by D. Appleton & Co. 1876.
"PLUTARCH's Lives."
EDITH RALPH's "Step by Step Through the Bible."
GIBBON's "Decline and Fall of the Roman Empire."
GOODRICH's "Roman History."
CHARLES DICKENS' "Child's History of England."
MARY FORD's "Child's History of Rome."
PETER PARLEY's "Cabinet Library." (1849.)
BARNES' "General History."
MAHAFFY's "History of Civilization."
NIEBUHR's "Stories of Greece."
BULFINCH's Mythology.
GUERBER's "Greek Stories."
FRANCILLON's "Gods and Heroes."
BROOK's "Iliad" and "Odyssey."
LAMB's "Adventure of Ulysses."
Cox's Mythology.
CHURCH's "Stories of Homer."
KINGSLEY's "Greek Heroes."
BUTTERWORTH's "Zigzag Journeys," by Estes & Lauriat.
LYDIA HOYT FARMER's "Boys' Book of Famous Rulers," by T. Y. Crowell & Co.
HENRY A. FORD's "Poems of History."
Poems from Byron, Bryant, Macaulay, Cowper
"Life of Paul," from Bible.
Encyclopedia Britannica.

www.ingramcontent.com/pod-product-compliance
Lightning Source LLC
Chambersburg PA
CBHW020827230426
43666CB00007B/1135